Learning Disabilities

Teaching-Learning Strategies

Rashmi Agrawal

BVLN Rao

SHIPRA

(2020 PoD, First Published 2010)

Rs. 850, US$ 34

ISBN: 978- ISBN: 978-81-7541-568-3

2023 Impression, PoD

Learning Disabilities: Teaching-Learning Strategies

Published by:
SHIPRA PUBLICATIONS
LG 18-19, Pankaj Central Market
I.P. Ext., Patparganj, Delhi 110092, Ind
Tel.: +91 11 2223 5152; 96500 28065
E-mail: info@shiprapublication.com
www.shiprapublication.com

Preface

When a child did not learn at the pace the other children learned, it used to be considered as lacking in intelligence, or parents and teachers thought he was not paying enough attention towards his studies. In recent times, however, the concept of learning disabilities has been recognized. It is now accepted that some children do not learn as quickly as their peers because they suffer from some or the other of learning disorders. A child may excel in music or painting but not in mathematics or English. This may be due to a learning disorder. At the same time, this problem cannot be attributed to only learning disability. In other words, lack of learning on the part of child may or may not be due to a learning disorder. Moreover, the child suffering from learning disability may have problems in learning in one specific area and may excel in other areas. The recognition of this fact calls for a change in strategy of teaching-learning process and the attitude of the teachers and parents towards the learning disabled child.

This book is an attempt to take a comprehensive look at the learning disabilities and the strategies to tackle them. It starts from defining the concept of learning disabilities with special reference to dyslexia, which is more common among the children, and goes on to describe the various forms of learning disabilities. The book then peeps into the past and takes a look at the historical background of learning disability and surveys the researches that are going on to delve deep into the subject. As has been mentioned, every child who is slow in learning need not be a learning disabled child. Therefore, the book provides inputs on how a learning disabled child can be identified by parents and the school, indicating the facilities available for diagnosis of learning disabilities. The causes of learning disabilities, which include genetic and environmental factors, have been discussed. Impact of learning disabilities on children, the specific problems of learning disabled, their educational problems, etc. have been discussed in the book in detail.

The book is a practical guide in explaining what teaching learning strategies can be adopted to teach the learning disabled. Parents, teachers and therapists would find it useful in dealing with the learning disabled children. The book also explains what can be done at school and community level to deal with such children. The intervention options have been detailed.

Comments on the book are welcome.

Authors are extremely grateful to Shipra Publications for their constant support and motivation to develop the book on such a socially relevant area.

Contents

Learning Disabilities with Reference to Dyslexia

LEARNING DISABILITIES

It is common knowledge that some children learn faster than others. One would see a child absorbing all mathematical theorems without much effort either on his or teacher's part, while another needs hours and hours of explanation and practice to gain even a part of that knowledge. Or a child goes on pronouncing or spelling words wrongly, even if the text is simple and the child has had occasion to practice those words several times before. The reasons why it is so have always attracted the attention of educationalists and psychologists. In the past, the easy explanation had generally been that the child learning slowly was less intelligent than others or that he did not pay adequate attention to studies or did not practice hard enough. While such reasons hold good in many cases even today, new knowledge has shown that it need not always be so. It is not always that the slow learning is due to lack of adequate intelligence or proper work habits on the part of the child. The problem lies elsewhere. Modern researches identified certain learning disorders or learning disabilities among certain children which affect their learning process in some areas like listening, speaking, writing or arithmetic, even though there are arguments as to what causes these disorders. More on this will be said later in the book. This chapter tries to explain the concepts and definitions of such learning disorders.

A learning disability is a generic term referring to difficulties in the acquisition and use of listening, speaking, reading, writing, reasoning or mathematical abilities.

Children with learning disabilities are also known as 'slow—learners'. Generally, the teachers consider these children as mentally retarded. But that is not a correct assumption. These slow learners are not necessarily mentally retarded children but suffer from some or the other problem. These problems could be due to difficulty in memorizing, writing, or concentrating. Some Children may have difficulty in reading or they may lack motor coordination. These children with learning difficulty are to be identified. Generally these children have normal or sometimes even above average intelligence.

DEFINITIONS

Learning disabilities have been defined as "a disorder in one or more of the basic psychological processes involved in understanding or in using language, spoken or written, that may manifest itself in imperfect ability to listen, think, speak, read, write, spell or to do mathematical calculations. The term includes such conditions as perceptual disabilities, brain injury, minimal brain dysfunction, dyslexia, and developmental aphasia. The term does not apply to children who have learning problems that are primarily the result of visual, hearing or motor disabilities, of mental retardation, of emotional disturbance, or of environmental, cultural, or economic disadvantage" (National Advisory Committee, USA, 1969).

Kirk, S.A. states that "The term learning disability is not meant to be used for children with minor or temporary difficulties in learning but with a severe discrepancy between abilities and achievements in educational performance and such severe discrepancies described as learning difficulties with significant learning problems that cannot be explained by mental retardation, sensory impairment, emotional disturbance or lack of opportunity to learn."

National Centre for Learning Disabilities defines learning disability as "a neurological disorder that affects the brains ability to receive, process, store and respond to information. The term learning disability is used to describe the seeming unexplained difficulty a person of at least average intelligence has in acquiring basic academic skills."

The definitions show that:

1. Learning disabilities are not the same as mental retardation.

2. It is due to some damage of the brain or dysfunction of the nervous system.
3. Academic performance is not according to the intelligence of the child.
4. The disability may show in the process of learning in one or more areas such as writing, speech, learning maths, or language, etc.
5. Learning disability is manifested in different ways in different people.
6. Learning disorders may lead to socio-emotional and behaviour difficulties.

Golick (1970) has classified learning disabilities in the following categories.

- Poor body awareness – child cannot locate various body parts, difficulty in telling between right and left.
- Poor ability to combine vision and movement – poor eye-hand coordination.
- Visual inefficiency – Even with normal vision, child may not be able to give selective vision.
- Poor listening ability – easily distracted towards noise.
- Poor integration of information from sensory channels – child is not able to integrate the alphabets with their sounds.
- Poor grasp of sequence – child is not able to remember the sequence of things like counting from 1 to 10, which he will not count in order.
- Poor sense of rhythm – difficulty in narrating a poem.
- Problems with concepts – child has difficulty in identifying the similarities and variations in various objects. Poor concepts of time or number.
- Problems in learning – like difficulty in arithmetic, remembering numbers or names, difficulty, specially in memorizing.
- Poor general knowledge – child has difficulty in learning general information like home address, occupation of parents, names of friends, etc.

SUMMARY TABLE OF LEARNING DISABILITIES

Category	*Conditions*	*Examples*
1. Visual Problems	Poor visual memory	Not remembering faces, words, people's names, reversals in writing (41 instead of 14)
	Poor visual perception	Difficulty in seeing the difference between similar objects (b and d)
	Figure ground discrimination	Inability to find the place to write one's name on an application form
	Poor visual tracking	Inability to follow a line on a page
2. Auditory Problems	Poor auditory memory	Difficulty in remembering what has been said, information or instructions
	Poor auditory discrimination	Difficulties in telling the difference between similar sounds, e.g. bee and pea or seventy and seventeen
	Poor auditory sequencing	Confusion with number sequence, lists or directions
	Poor auditory figure ground	Trouble hearing sounds over background noises
3. Motor Problems	Poor eye-hand coordination	Difficulties with handwriting
	Poor small muscle control	Misjudging where to place things
	Poor large muscle control	Clumsiness
4. Organisational Problems	Poor time management	Inability to be punctual, to meet deadlines
	Poor ability to organize tasks	Not understanding the steps required to carry out a task
	Poor ability to organize space	Inability to arrange things in a cupboard, a desk, arranging matter in a page
	Impairment of executive function	Unable to analyse things or apply information in a new situation
5. Conceptual Problems	Difficulty in interpreting non-verbal language	Facial expressions or body language

(*Contd.*)

Category	*Conditions*	*Examples*
	Difficulty in understanding figures of speech	Idioms, metaphors, similies
	Difficulties in anticipating future	Doing things without assessing consequences
	Rigid thinking	Unable to be flexible in thinking
	Poor social skills and peer relations	Not maintaining eye contact during conversation, using inappropriate tone or language, lacking social graces

It may be mentioned that a person with learning disabilities in one area may be very successful in other areas.

DYSLEXIA

Manu was a very active child. He used to play cricket with his father and other friends. He used to think very creatively, had his own interesting ideas and narrated stories to his younger sister. When he got admitted to the school, initially every thing was all right as it was a play school. There were no books in the play school. In the play school he learnt a number of rhymes and sang them. He was a happy child.

His problem started once he was supposed to read. While other children of his age could learn to read, he could not. Parents got worried. Teachers earlier thought that the child was mischievous and very naughty. When punishment as well as persuasion did not help, he was referred to the school counselor. The counselor administered some psychological test to measure his IQ and other capabilities like visual perception, achievements in written work as well as diagnostic tests for dyslexia. The IQ of the Manu was above average but he was not able to perform according to his IQ. This discrepancy along with other diagnostic tests indicated that he was dyslexic.

Manu was able to speak fluently, but when it came to reading and writing he faced difficulty. The child grew up but was still reversing some of his letters and had difficulty with directions, doing puzzles, etc. His parents were unable to accept that their child was dyslexic.

THE DEFINITIONS

Dyslexia is a specific learning disability in the area of reading and writing. The term is derived from the Greek word "dys" (meaning poor or inadequate) and "lexis" (words or language).

A person with learning disability is someone with average or above average intelligence whose difficulty in reading, writing and/ or spelling is not the result of emotional problems, lack of motivation, poor teaching, mental retardation, or vision/hearing deficits. Rather, it is neurologically—based and tends to run in families.

Dyslexia has been defined in several ways from a simple perspective to complex perspective. These perspectives have evolved on the basis of various researches. These researches have been conducted keeping in focus the behavioural aspects, cognitive aspects and physiological aspects. The behavioural researches take into account the ability with performance particularly in respect of reading, writing and spelling. Cognitive theorists look at working memory deficit or poor short-term memory and processing difficulties with auditory and/or visual information. The biological/ neurological researchers try to observe the differences in the way the brain is formed and how it functions and the relationship between the left and right hemispheres of the brain.

Some of the definitions used to define dyslexia have been given below:

British Psychological Society,(1999): Dyslexia is evident when accurate and fluent reading and/or spelling develops very incompletely or with great difficulty. This focuses on literacy learning at the word level and implies that the problem is severe and persistent despite appropriate learning opportunities. It provides the basis for a staged process of assessment through teaching. and implies that the problem is severe and persistent despite appropriate learning opportunities. It provides the basis for a staged process of assessment through teaching.

British Dyslexia Association,(2000) said Dyslexia is a combination of abilities and difficulties, which affect the learning process in one or more of reading, spelling and writing activities. Accompanying weaknesses may also be seen in speed of processing, short-term memory, sequencing, auditory and visual perception, spoken language and motor skills.

Crombie, (2002) Dyslexia is a difficulty with literacy, which results in a person requiring a set of accommodations to be made to enable them to demonstrate their abilities. Accommodations here can be defined as a set of enabling arrangements, which are put in place to ensure that the dyslexic person can demonstrate their strengths and abilities and show attainment.

The World Federation of Neurologists defined (1968) dyslexia is "a disorder in children who, despite conventional classroom experience, fail to attain the language skills of reading, writing, and spelling commensurate with their intellectual abilities."

U.S. National Institutes of Health, dyslexia is a learning disability that can hinder a person's ability to read, write, spell, and sometimes speak. It is the most common learning disability in children, which continues throughout the life. The severity of dyslexia can vary from mild to severe. It is important to identify the problem at an early stage so that treatment could be provided. However children with this learning disability can be helped to develop language skills at any stage.

British Dyslexia Association,(1968), "A complex neurological condition which is constitutional in origin. The symptoms may affect various areas of learning and function and may be described as a specific difficulty in reading, spelling and written language. One or more of these areas may be affected: numeracy, notational skills (music), motor function and organisational skills. However, it is particularly related to mastering written language, although oral language may be affected to some degree."

A more recent definition of dyslexia has been given by International Association of Dyslexia 'Dyslexia is a neurologically—based, often familial, disorder which interferes with the acquisition and processing of language. Varying in degrees of severity, it is manifested by difficulties in receptive and expressive language, including phonological processing, in reading, writing, spelling, handwriting, and sometimes in arithmetic. Dyslexia is not the result of lack of motivation, sensory impairment, inadequate instructional or environmental opportunities, or other limiting conditions, but may occur together with these conditions. Although dyslexia is lifelong, individuals with dyslexia frequently respond successfully to timely and appropriate intervention.'

The term dyslexia covers a range of symptoms and learning difficulties related to the written word. About 10 per cent of the world's population, regardless of nationality, income level, sex, race or IQ has dyslexia. Dyslexic people are visual thinkers. But they find it difficult to understand letters, numbers, symbols or written words, which lead to problems with reading or writing. Mathematics is also out of bound for them. It is difficult for them to focus their attention.

As is evident from the above example, the dyslexic child has average or above average intelligence. He is not mentally retarded as sometimes is considered. He is neither stupid nor "lazy".

Some children with dyslexia have Attention Deficit Disorder also along with dyslexia and therefore find it difficult to concentrate for a long time on one topic. Their minds always move from one issue to another: they keep involved in thinking of something or the other. They do not remember teaching in the school. They understand only a few points as at other times they might be thinking something else, which leaves gaps in their knowledge.

When a child starts learning to read or write he tries to learn through a combination of visuals and sounds. He matches the sound with the letter. This involves "decoding" skills. He learns to recognize letters visually and connect these with the sound that each letter makes. Afterwards he learns to recognize the letter and sound and understands how they form words. A child with dyslexia typically has trouble making the connection between the sound and the letter that makes that sound and difficulty in associating sounds with words. It is very difficult for him to read long sentences. A child with dyslexia easily forgets meaning of the words/sentences or paragraph.

Sometimes a dyslexic child cannot differentiate between certain sounds which appear alike such as 'P' and 'B,' or letters that have similarity like 'g', 'q'. He can also forget the correct sequencing of letters or numbers. Reversed numbers or letters are also not understood properly by the dyslexic child. To him 'was' appears like 'saw.' It is wrong to think that every child who has this problem is dyslexic. In earlier learning stages many children can have this problem but if this problem continues then the child should be sent for diagnosis.

THE HISTORICAL BACKGROUND

- Dyslexia was identified in 1881 by Dr. Oswald Berkhan.
- In 1887 Rudolf Berlin, an ophthalmologist used it to refer

to a case of a young boy who had a severe impairment in learning to read and write in spite of his intellectual and physical abilities.

- In 1896, W. Pringle Morgan, a physician, from England published an artcle on a learning disorder with specific reference to reading titled "Congenital Word Blindness". The article mentioned the case of a 14-year-old boy who was not able to read while he had normal intelligence and was normal in other activities also.
- During early 1900s, James Hinshelwood, a British ophthalmologist, published a series of articles in medical journals relating to cases of congenital word blindness. He said that the primary disability was in visual memory for words and letters, and described symptoms including letter reversals, and difficulties with spelling and reading comprehension.
- In 1925, Samuel T. Orton began studying reading difficulties and determined that there was a syndrome unrelated to brain damage that made learning to read difficult. Orton called the condition strephosymbolia (meaning 'twisted signs'). He theorised that individuals with dyslexia had difficulty associating the visual forms of words with their spoken forms. The Orton—Gillingham approach to remedial reading instruction is still widely used and forms the basis of many reading intervention programmes.
- Based on various researches during middle of 1930s it was brought out that in all the subjects, the words were not perceived in their globality but required a meticulous analysis of the letters and syllables. (Dearborn, Gates, Bennet and Blau, Tinker and Goodenough). A number of experiments were conducted to understand typology of Dyslexia.
- In the 1970s, a new hypothesis emerged. It was based on Orton's theories. The new Hypothsis was that dyslexia stems from a deficit in phonological processing or difficulty in recognizing that spoken words are formed by discrete sounds. For example, the word CAT comes from the sounds [k], [æ], and [t]). As a result, affected individuals have difficulty associating these sounds with the visual letters that make up written words. This research suggested that

phonological awareness instruction can improve decoding skills for children with reading difficulties.

- The advent of neuro-imaging techniques to study brain structure and function brought out new understanding about dyslexia during the period 1980s and 1990s. Current models of the relation between the brain and dyslexia generally focus on some form of defective or delayed brain maturation.
- Researches are currently on to find a link between the neurological and genetic characteristics findings on one hand, and the reading disorder on the other. There are many theories of dyslexia, but most researches show that, whatever the biological cause, dyslexia is a matter of reduced phonogical awareness, the ability to analyze and link the units of spoken and written languages.

TYPES OF DYSLEXIA

Several types of dyslexia have been identified which are detailed below: One classification is on the basis of its causes:

1. *Trauma dyslexia:* It usually occurs after some form of brain trauma or injury to the area of the brain that controls reading and writing.
2. *Primary dyslexia:* This type of dyslexia is a dysfunction or damage to the left side of the brain, which is termed as cerebral cortex. It is not affected by age. In other words children with this type of dyslexia cannot go beyond fourth—grade level. Even when they grow they find it difficult to read, spell, and or write. Primary dyslexia is hereditary. It is found more often in boys than in girls.
3. *Secondary or "developmental dyslexia':* This type of dyslexia is caused by hormonal development during the early stages of fetal development. Developmental dyslexia diminishes as the child matures. It has been seen that it is more common in boys.

The other classification of dyslexia is on the basis of functions one performs and difficulty in performing those functions:

1. *Visual dyslexia:* In this type of dyslexia the child is unable

to handle number and letter reversals and write symbols in the correct sequence.

2. *Auditory dyslexia:* In auditory dyslexia child has difficulty with sounds of letters or groups of letters. Either the child mixes up the sounds or feels that he has not heard it properly. The sounds are perceived as jumbled.
3. *Dysgraphia:* It refers to the child's difficulty in holding and controlling a pencil and therefore he cannot write the words on paper correctly.

To summarise

- Dyslexia is one of the most common learning disabilities.
- Dyslexia relates to difficulty in learning to read and write.
- Dyslexia can be related to brain injury, hereditary, or hormonal influences.
- Letter and number reversals are a common warning sign of dyslexia.
- Diagnosis of dyslexia involves reviewing the child's processing of information from seeing, hearing, and participating in activities.
- Treatment of dyslexia ideally involves planning between the parent(s) and the teachers.

LEARNING DISABILITY AND INDIAN SCENARIO

In India Learning disability has been identified as such only in the very recent past. Earlier, it was thought that the inability of the child who is unable to learn is due to his lack of attention or due to not giving adequate time towards the studies. With the growing awareness about learning disorders globally, India has also started recognizing the fact that lack of learning could be due to learning disorders. This awareness has sensitized the schools, parents as well as the society. The maximum gainer of this recognition is the child who is suffering from some or the other learning disorder. Learning disability is an invisible disorder that presents the fullest growth of the child disabilities and potential, and which poses a threat to the development of the nation's human resources, if not recognized. It has been estimated globally that about 14 per cent of all school children suffer from some or the other learning disability. Even after the growing awareness about the factual position of the disabilities, most of the schools in the country are not well equipped to deal with these disorders.

Samir Parekh, a child psychiatrist says that learning disability is not a disease as such. It is a life long difficulty which poses various challenges in a person's life. But these challenges can be tackled with the support of the society as a whole. In this country clarity is still awaited about various learning disabilities, their assessment and process of diagnosis, the extent of the problem etc. Indian children differ from those of the western world. India has its own socio—economic and cultural scenario. Moreover, even within the country, these socio-economic and cultural factors vary from one part of the country to the other. In various remote areas, people are not even exposed to modern world which is also a factor contributing to learning disability. Substantial researches and understanding is needed in the concept of learning disabilities prevailing in the country and the factors responsible for it. Identification of learning disabilities has to be area specific and approaches to tackle the problem have to be addressed keeping the unique factors of socio-economic and cultural variations of the country in focus.

Most of the time dyslexia and learning disabilities are seen as synonyms. Central Board of Secondary Education in New Delhi has recognized dyslexia as impairment. Other disabilities like locomotor disability, hearing disability, vision disability, cerebral palsy, thalassemia, dyslexia and aphasia are some of the other disabilities which have been recognized in the country. Even after the recognition of learning disabilities, no policy on learning disorders has been adopted so far in India. This is one of the major reasons that schools are not able to provide an environment for the children with learning disorders. The concept of inclusive education as although has been introduced in the country, the children with learning disabilities are not being rehabilitated in normal schools. Generally, schools do not give admissions to the learning disabled especially private owned schools. Even when the child with learning disability gets admission his disability is generally ignored and he is vulnerable to punishment for not performing. Rehabilitation Council of India, Ministry of Human Resource Development and Ministry of Social Justice and Empowerment have to come together to help the learning disabled, especially, in the area of identification of such children. But there is a long way to go till the learning disabled children are really helped. Some of the organizations like ORKIDS in New Delhi, Samveda Research and Training Centre, Kolkata, Tata Interactive Learning Disability Forum in Mumbai and Kolkata are some of the organizations that are committed to the cause of education with special reference to learning disorders. (A list of organizations in Delhi and other states and resource centres helping disabled has been annexed.

Efforts on the side of government and other agencies are leading to positive results. In some of the states concessions such as reducing the number of examination papers, less homework, more time to complete the paper etc. are being provided to learning disabled children.

Various Forms of Learning Disabilities

Learning disabilities are a group of disabilities relating to reading, writing and showing slow achievements and progress. The child can suffer from one or more learning disabilities. Some forms of learning disabilities are detailed below:

DYSCALCULIA

This type of learning disability is related to mathematical operations. The difficulities in mathematical calculations may vary from individual to individual. Some children with difficulty in mathematical calculations may overcome their problems with time and if special attention is paid to them, while in cases of others it could be a life long disability. The child suffering with dyscalculia may not be able to remember numbers or solving the mathematical problem in a sequential manner. Some other children may have problems with spatial relationships and may find it difficult to solve geometrical problems. Other children may have trouble in speaking and writing and may face a different kind of problem in solving mathematical questions which involve language processing. Thus, children suffering from dyscalculia may have varying problems in learning the numbers, sequencing, sorting of objects involving various shapes and sizes, distinguishing various colours, recognizing various patterns and handling questions which involve comparison between two or more objects. At a younger age, these children also find it difficult to remember counting, reversing the numbers, matching the numbers or finding odd numbers out. When children grow and the mathematics also becomes complex, they find it difficult to do even the basic tasks, which are addition, substraction, multiplication and division. They are not able to remember tables, so it is very difficult for them to do basic mathematical calculations. Obviously with these difficulties, advanced mathematical applications are difficult for them. It may, however, be kept in mind here that aptitude for mathematical ability differs. Children with high aptitude for mathematics can learn very fast as compared to others who have a low aptitude. Thus, those who learn slow may not necessarily be suffering from dyscalculia.

To identify the children with dyscalculia, a pencil paper-test can be given or the child can be asked to do simple mathematical calculations mentally. The evaluation would facilitate understanding the actual level of skill of mathematics in the child. Some simple exercises like counting the money or objects, scoring while playing, giving them the directions, etc. are useful to identify such children.

DYSGRAPHIA

Dysgraphia is related to difficulties in writing. Children suffering from dysgraphia are unable to write words properly on a given line. Dysgraphia is of two types-one relates to those who have visual spatial problems and the other relates to language processing. The children who have difficulty with spatial relationships cannot process the visuals. While the children with language processing difficulty can not make out what they really hear. Initially, the children find it difficult to hold and control a pencil or pen to write the words on paper correctly. Their grip and body position is not proper. They also cannot recognize the various shapes and, therefore, the writing of letters is difficult for them. They do not understand the upper or lower case of letters and have no consistency in giving spaces between two words. They try to avoid the writing tasks. When the children grow, it is difficult to deciphed their handwriting. Sometimes, they speak loud when they write. They cannot coordinate with their thinking and writing. They leave a word or a sentence in between or they omit certain words. As a result, it is difficult for them to sequence their thoughts and understand grammar. These signs can be observed in the early years and the children of dysgraphia can be diagnosed.

DYSPRAXIA

Dyspraxia is related to motor skill development of the children. This difficulty generally occurs along with some other learning disabilities discussed, and affects the basic functions of the person in his daily routine tasks. There are four categories of dyspraxia:

(i) Ideomotor Dyspraxia: Children suffering from this kind of disability are unable to do simple tasks which involve a single step. For example, the child is unable to comb his hairs or wave hand, etc.

(ii) Ideation Dyspraxia: In this kind of dyspraxia, the child is unable to do the tasks which have more than one step such as putting on clothes, brushing, etc.

(iii) Oromotor Dyspraxia: The person suffering with this disability finds it difficult to coordinate movement of musles which help in speaking.

(iv) Constructional Dyspraxia: In this disability, the person is unable to visualize the spatial relationships; therefore, he cannot keep the things in correct positions or move the object from one place to another place.

At a very young age, children suffering with dyspraxia find it difficult to walk or jump or say simple words. They get easily frustrated and irritated by touch of skin. When the children grow and start going to school they find it difficult to establish coordination of various parts of their bodies needed to perform a number of activities like holding a pen, buttoning up the clothes, playing, and speaking. When the problem persists to older ages, the grown up children have difficulty in writing, driving, face problems in speech control and become sensitive to touch, taste, smells and lights. Assessment of dyspraxia is extremely essential at the early stages of life to help the child in leading a normal life.

DYSLEXIA

Dyslexia as explained elsewhere in the book, is one of the learning disabilities that is generally related to the difficulty in learning to read. The child suffering from dyslexia finds it difficult to read even simple words. He mixes up the letters in a word; may not be able to speak what he has read; he may invent his own spellings of words. Dyslexia has two sub-types one is known as surface dyslexia and the other is phonological dyslexia. Surface dyslexia refers to poor lexical abilities. The individual with this type of dyslexia cannot read out loud using lexical process, which involves speaking a word through the use of a past word already learned. Phonological dyslexia has been defined by Castles, and Coltheart (1993) as a disability which is characterized by subjects who can read aloud both regular and irregular words but have difficulties with non words and with connecting sounds to symbols or with sounding out words. Dyslexs generally suffer from this sub-type of dyslexia. In phonology, the sounds are combined together to produce words. A child suffering from phonological disorder may produce the sound but may use this sound at a wrong position. For example he may use the sound of 'T' for the alphabet 'G' or the sound 'F' for the alphabet 'S'. They may also confuse in sequencing the sound correctly in pronouncing the words. Dyslexia has to be identified and treated in time. It does not however, hamper the career prospects of a person. A number of academicians in various fields, sports, politics suffer from dyslexia.

READING AND WRITING PROCESSING DISRUPTIONS

The human brain has an innate capacity for spoken language. The following is the process of reading and writing.

- A word is seen by the eyes.
- Eyes relay the letters to the brain.
- Brain matches the letters to the sounds they represent.
- Brain combines the separate sounds into a single sound.
- Brain uses long-term memory to see what that sound represents in order to bring up the image of the word read.

Any disruption in this function relates to the learning disability.

INFORMATION PROCESSING DIFFICULTIES

There are four components of information processing. These components are inputs which are received by the child through the use of senses. Any disruption in any of the senses may cause disruption in receiving the information. For example problems in taking inputs through auditory sense can pose problems in taking inputs through this sense and one may not be able to distinguish in various voices; Integration is second component where information received is integrated through sequencing, categorization, interpretation etc. Third component is storage which relates to memory and the last component is output in which information is recalled wherever needed. Disruption at any of these stages may be a cause of learning disability. These difficulties can be of classified as Auditory processing disorders and visual processing disorders. In Auditory Processing Disorders the child has difficulty in making distinction in various sounds while in visual Processing Disorders the child may find it difficult to interpret visual information such as reading maps, charts, symbols, etc.

SOME OTHER RELATED DISABILITIES THAT AFFECT TEACHING–LEARNING

There are some other disabilities which are not learning disabilities as such but create hinderance in teaching learning. Here two such disabilities are discussed—one is Attention Deficit Hyperactivity Disorder and another is Autism.

ATTENTION DEFICIT HYPERACTIVITY DISORDER (ADHD)

ADHD as such is not a learning disability, but children with ADHD face difficulty in learning. ADHD indirectly affects teaching—learning process. Children with ADHD are hyperactive and therefore they need some or the other activity to do. They cannot remain idle, change their seats from place to another and need new activities. They get bored easily while doing one activity for a long time. This is the reason, they may find it difficult to focus their attention on studies and concentrate on the teaching in the class. Their behaviour is uncontrolled and unpredictable.

Child with ADHD can be identified at the age 5 to 7. Parents and teachers can identify the child through the following symptoms:

- Impulsive behaviour
- Restlessness
- Lack of attention on instructions
- Lack of concentration for a long time
- Extra-ordinarily active (hyperactive)

American Psychiatric Association (2000) has listed certain symptoms; on that basis three types of ADHD have been explained.

1. Inattentive Type

In Inattentive type of ADHD, children lack concentration. They do things too fast without understanding or going into details. They cannot concentrate on any thing for a long time, therefore, do not work according to the instructions given in the school or home. They perform their own way and so do not organize their things and activities properly. Their attention gets distracted on even a very minor disruption or thought. They forget their things here and there and cannot remember where their things are?

2. Hyperactive Impulsive Type

Children with this type of ADHD are highly active; they do not think before acting and are very impulsive. They immediately react on an even a small provocation. They put themselves in difficult situations or in danger. They may climb a mountain without understanding the path of going and coming back. They can open toys or other equipments to see them what is inside or to repair them without knowing how to do. They may run on the street without seeing the traffic. They do not understand the repercussions of their impulsive behaviour. They may repent later as they do not know how to deal with difficult situations they have put themselves into. Such children can be identified by their following behaviours:

- Constant running, climbing or doing some or the other activity which may not be desirable.
- Disobeying instructions like not sitting or doing work when they are supposed to.
- Interrupt or talk too much while playing with friends or even with self.
- Have no patience for being in the queues and wait for their turn.
- Make interruption when others are talking.

3. Combine Type

ADHD children in this type have behaviour of both the types of ADHD explained above. The main behaviours are extra-ordinary activity and impulsive behaviour which leave them extra-ordinary anxious and sometimes depressed.

How to Deal with ADHD Child

At the first step child should be identified for his ADHD behaviours. Normal curriculum in the school will not help the child. Special programmes have to be devised according to the needs of the individuals. More activities that involve newness and innovation have to be planned for such children. The activities should be of short-term duration as these children may not be able to concentrate on one activity for a long time. Special education teacher helps such students. The causes of ADHD are still unknown. But it has been researched that neuro-transmitters which is a chemical in the brain is in low amount in ADHD children. These chemicals of the brain lead to controlled behaviour in the children.

AUTISM

Autism is a type of neural development disorder. In this disorder, child finds it difficult to communicate with others appropriately. He also has problem in social interaction and making friends. Autism is a lifelong disorder that interferes with the ability to understand what is seen, heard, and touched. This can cause profound problems in personal behaviour and in the ability to relate to others. A person with autism must learn how to communicate normally and how to relate to people, objects, and events. Autism can be diagnosed at an early age of three years. Symptoms of autism can be observed when a child is six months old. Following symptoms can be observed in an autism child.

- Impairement in social interaction
- Impairement in communication
- Repetitive behaviour
- Lack of interests in various things. Child has a few friends and limited interests

Autism can take place in variety of ways showing a combination of symptoms. According to the APA, they may include any combination of the following in varying degrees of severity:

- insistence on sameness; resistance to change
- difficulty in expressing needs; using gestures or pointing instead of words
- repeating words or sentences instead of using normal, responsive language
- laughing, crying, showing distress for reasons not apparent to others
- aloof behaviour, seeking solitude
- tantrums
- refusal to cuddle or be cuddled
- little or no eye contact
- unresponsiveness to normal teaching methods
- sustained odd play
- inappropriate attachments to objects
- apparent over-sensitivity or under-sensitivity to pain
- no fear of danger
- uneven gross/fine motor skills
- not responsive to verbal cues; acts as if deaf although hearing tests in normal range

The causes of autism are not very clear. It has been linked with genetic factors. Sometimes it can be due to defects at birth. Environmental factors such as pesticides, use of drugs and medicines, heavy metals, pollutents etc also are responsible for autism. Further studies point to major disturbances in the body chemistry of children with autism. Disruption is most often found in fatty acid metabolism, electrolyte balances, problems with digestive functioning, production of red and white blood cells, and the body's balance of minerals. Allergies also cause autism in some children. Autism affects the way in which the brain uses or transmits information. Studies have found abnormalities in several parts of the brains of those with autism that almost certainly occurred during fetal development.

Asperger syndrome is another form of autism. Autism can be classified in three types depending upon the extent of functionality of the child. These three types are:

- Low functioning autism
- Medium functioning autism
- High functioning autism

This classification as such is not very rigid or standardized but helps in providing and deciding amount of care one needs.

How to Diagnose Autism

Autism is diagnosed by case study method where developmental history of the child is recorded. It is followed by observing and evaluating the child's behaviour, communication skills, and social interactions. Medical tests are not generally needed for autism.

A number of psychological tests and scales are available that are used to diagnose autistic child. Some the these used in developed countries are as below.

- Childhood Autism Rating Scale (CARS). CARS is based on observed behaviour. Using a 15-point scale, professionals evaluate a child's relationship to people, body use, adaptation to change, listening response, and verbal communication.
- Checklist for Autism in Toddlers (CHAT). CHAT is used to screen for autism at 18 months of age. The screening tool uses a short questionnaire with two sections, one prepared by the parents, the other by the child's family doctor or pediatrician.
- Autism Screening Questionnaire (ASQ). The ASQ is a 40-item screening scale used with children four and older to help evaluate communication skills and social functioning.
- Screening Test for Autism in Two-Year Olds. This test uses direct observations to study behavioural features in children under two. It is focused on three skills areas, play, motor imitation, and joint attention that are associated with autism.

How to Deal with Autistic Child

Nutrition: There is often a strong nutritional dysfunction involved in autism. A major overhaul of the child's diet should be done. A healthy diet of whole foods with no preservatives or additives including food dyes, is recommended. Processed foods such as white flour, white sugar, margarine, and hydrogenated fats should be avoided because they interfere with the stability of blood chemistry.

Tests should be done to see the blood levels of chemicals in the body. Diet is needed for changing the chemical imbalances. Possible gut and immune system dysfunction should also be addressed.

Treatment and Intervention

Most experts recommend a complex treatment regimen for autism that begins early in life and continues through the teenage years. Behavioural therapies are used in conjunction with medications and special diets. Because the symptoms vary so widely from one person to the next, there is not a single approach that works best for every person. Interventions include special training in music, listening, vision, speech and language, and senses. Sensory integration training may be used to normalize sensory functions. Training to change aberrant behaviours should be started as early in the autistic child's life as possible, since early intervention appears to have the most influence on brain development and functioning. A child with autism is able to learn best in a specialized, structured programme that emphasizes individualized instruction. Allopathic medicines should be used only after consultation with the Doctor.

Studies show that people with autism can improve significantly with proper treatment. While there is no cure, the negative behaviours of autism can be made to improve. Behaviour therapies are specially helpful for interventions which is based on learning theories. The technique uses reinforcement procedures to increase on-task behaviour and social interactions; teaching new skills (functional life skills, communication skills, or social skills); maintaining desirable behaviours (teaching self-control and self-monitoring procedures to maintain social skills); transferring behaviour from one situation or response to another (from completing assignments in the resource room to performing as well in the mainstream classroom); reducing interfering behaviours (e.g., self-injury).

Specific educational/behavioural therapy programmes for the treatment of autism include

- The Miller Method. The Miller Method extensively uses adaptive equipment, including platforms (to elevate the child so as to help increase eye contact), large swinging balls (to expand the child's reality system) and Swiss cheese boards (to teach motor planning, as well as to increase the child's understanding of his or her relation to environment and space).
- Discrete Trial Training (DTT). DTT methodology has been linked to make a balance between the large amount of information and interaction that typically confronts the child with autism. Under this method the information is presented in small quantity.
- Treatment and Education of Autistic and Communication Handicapped Children (TEACCH). The TEACCH approach includes a focus on the person with autism and development of a programme around this person's skills, interests, and needs. The programme is individual focused.
- The Son-Rise programme. The Son-Rise programme ranges from one week to six months and is designed to teach parents, professionals, and support staff of children with a wide range of disabilities how to implement home-based programmes based upon the Kaufmans' theories of learning.
- Megavitamin therapy. Some studies have shown that vitamin B_6 improves eye contact and speech and lessens tantrum behaviour. Vitamin B_6 causes fewer side effects than other medications and is considered safe when used in appropriate doses. It should be taken after consulting a Doctor.

What Parents can Do

Parents can help their autistic child in the best manner. At the first instance they should learn more and more about the autism. As a next step they should mentally prepare themselves to deal with their autistic child without any stigma as they have to go to the Doctor and follow his advice. Care and concern is extremely required on the part of the parents.

Researches and Theories on Learning Disability

Specific interventions according to the child's specific problem can go a long way in improving the performance of the child. Although learning disabilities are a life long problem, researches have enabled identification of various types of interventions that have been helpful in dealing with different types of learning disabilities up to a great extent.

Being a recently recognized phenomenon, the issue of learning disabilities is increasingly drawing attention of social researchers. More than 250 researches have identified social skill characteristics that are different among the learning disabled in comparison with those of other children. Tanis Bryan is one of the pioneers who conducted researches on the issue of social competence of learning disabled. He stated that differences were found in the learning disabled and the non-learning disabled children in quality of communication. Learning disabled children were less assertive, less persuable and less interactive.

Scientists are studying the functioning of the brain and found out that neuroplasticity can come to the rescue of learning disorders. The term relates to the brain's ability to change to form new connections and generate new brain cells. This happens in response to the new experiences and learning that takes place in day to day life. Thus, neuroplasticity can help in retraining of the brain. Once it is established that the brain can change, learning disabilities relating to brain disorders can be tackled with new hope. The concept of neuroplasticity works like a telephone, as the faults in the connecting lines of the telephone can affect the telephone communication. It gets repaired if a new line is laid. Similarly, learning disability can get repaired with new neural connections.

Several theories of child development and learning have influenced discussions of school readiness. Three of them have had profound impact on kindergarten readiness practices. These three theories include the maturationist, environmentalist, and constructivist perspectives of development (Powell, 1991).

MATURATIONIST THEORY

The maturationist theory was advanced by the work of Arnold Gessell. Maturationists believe that development is a biological process that occurs automatically in predictable, sequential stages over time (Hunt, 1969). This perspective leads many educators and families to assume that young children will acquire knowledge naturally and automatically as they grow physically and become older, provided that they are healthy (Demarest, Reisner, Anderson, Humphrey, Farquhar, & Stein, 1993).

School readiness, according to maturationists, is a state at which all healthy young children arrive when they can perform tasks such as reciting the alphabet and counting; these tasks are required for learning more complex tasks such as reading and arithmetic. Because development and school readiness occur naturally and automatically, maturationists believe that the best practices for parents are to teach young children to recite the alphabet and count while being patient and waiting for children to become ready for kindergarten. If a child is developmentally unready for school, maturationists might suggest referrals to transitional kindergartens, retention, or holding children out of school for an additional year (DeCos, 1997). These practices are sometimes used by schools, educators, and parents when a young child developmentally lags behind his or her peers. The young child's underperformance is interpreted as the child needing more time to acquire the knowledge and skills needed to perform at the level of his or her peers.

ENVIRONMENTALIST THEORY

Theorists such as John Watson, B.F. Skinner, and Albert Bandura contributed greatly to the environmentalist perspective of development. Environmentalists believe that the child's environment shapes his/her learning and behaviour. In fact, human behaviour, development, and learning are thought of as reactions to the environment. This perspective leads many families, schools, and educators to assume that young children develop and acquire new knowledge by reacting to their surroundings.

Kindergarten readiness, according to the environmentalists, is the age or stage when young children can respond appropriately to the environment of the school and the classroom (e.g., rules and regulations, curriculum activities, positive behaviour in group settings, and directions and instructions from teachers and other adults in the school). The ability to respond appropriately to this environment is necessary for young children to participate in teacher-initiated learning activities. Success is dependent on the child following instructions from the teacher or the adult in the classroom. Many environmentalist-influenced educators and parents believe that young children learn best by rote activities, such as reciting the alphabet over and over, copying letters, and tracing numbers. This viewpoint finds expression in kindergarten classrooms, where young children are expected to sit at desks arranged in rows and to listen attentively to their teachers. At home, parents may provide their young children with workbooks containing such activities as coloring or tracing letters and numbers—activities that require little interaction between parent and child. When young children are unable to respond appropriately to the classroom and school environment, they often are labeled as having some form of learning disabilities and are tracked in classrooms with curriculum designed to control their behaviours and responses.

CONSTRUCTIVIST THEORY

The constructivist perspective of readiness and development was advanced by theorists such as Jean Piaget, Maria Montessori, and Lev Vygotsky. Although their work varies greatly, each articulates a similar context of learning and development. They are consistent in their belief that learning and development occur when young children interact with the environment and people around them (Hunt, 1969). Constructivists view young children as active participants in the learning process. In addition, constructivists believe young children initiate most of the activities required for learning and development. Because active interaction with the environment and people are necessary for learning and development, constructivists believe that children are ready for school when they can initiate many of the interactions they have with the environment and people around them.

Constructivist-influenced schools and educators pay a lot of attention to the physical environment and the curriculum of the early childhood classroom. Kindergarten classrooms often are divided into different learning centers and are equipped with developmentally appropriate materials for young children to play with and manipulate. Teachers and adults have direct conversations with children, children move actively from center to another, and daily activities are made meaningful through the incorporation of children's experiences into the curriculum. At home, parents engage their young children in reading and storytelling activities and encourage children's participation in daily household activities in a way that introduces such concepts as counting and language use. In addition, parents may provide young children with picture books containing very large print, and toys that stimulate interaction (such as building blocks and large puzzles). When a young child encounters difficulties in the learning process, the constructivist approach is neither to label the child nor to retain him or her; instead, constructivists give the child some individualized attention and customize the classroom curriculum to help the child address his or her difficulties.

Today, most researchers have come to understand that child development and the learning process takes place as articulated by the constructivists. However, this view has not been widely translated into practice. Many kindergarten teachers and parents still believe that young children are not ready for school unless they can recite the alphabet, count, and have the ability to follow instructions from adults.

THEORIES RELATING TO DYSLEXIA

Several theories have been propounded in relation to the specific learning disabilities in reading and writing, grouped under the term Dyslexia. These theories are of two broad types – (a) biological and (b) cognitive.

Biological theories of dyslexia describe dyslexic differences in terms of genetics and the structure of the brain. Theories of dyslexia that focus on the biological level underpin many other theories. Researchers who are exploring dyslexia at other levels may still acknowledge that biological differences are a factor. Many practitioners believe that dyslexic people often have relatives with the same condition. Genetic theories explore this possibility. Recent research into the structure of the brain in people with dyslexia suggests differences that might cause a range of effects, including visual perception difficulties.

The cognitive theories of dyslexia describe dyslexic difficulties in terms of the working of the brain. They focus on dyslexia as a difference in information processing – how the brain handles information coming to it through the senses. Educationalists see dyslexia principally as a difference at this level. This is not surprising given that learning depends on the ability to process information.

Some of the major theories which seek to explain the phenomenon of dyslexia are described below:

(a) The Evolutionary Hypothesis

This theory posits that reading is an unnatural act, and carried out by humans for an exceedingly brief period in our evolutionary history (Dalby, 1986). For example, it has been less than a hundred years that most western societies have promoted reading by the mass population and therefore the forces that shape our reading behaviour have been weak. Many areas of the world still do not have access to reading for the majority of the population. There is no evidence that "pathology" underlies dyslexia but much evidence for cerebral variation or differences. It is these essential differences that are taxed with the artificial task of reading.

(b) Phonological Processing Theory

Phonological processing is the ability to remember and assign the sounds associated with written letters and words. The phonological processing theory (also called phonolocial deficit theory) states that all the symptoms of dyslexia are caused by impairment in the ability to process written words into sounds. Most experts agree that difficulties in phonological processing play an important part in dyslexia. However, some argue that the difficulty in phonological processing is in fact a symptom, rather than the main cause of dyslexia.

The phonological hypothesis postulates that dyslexics have a specific impairment in the representation, storage and/or retrieval of speech sounds. It explains dyslexics' reading impairment on the basis that learning to read an alphabetic system requires learning the grapheme/phoneme correspondence, i.e. the correspondence between letters and constituent sounds of speech. If these sounds are poorly represented, stored or retrieved, the learning of grapheme/phoneme correspondences, the foundation of reading by phonic methods for alphabetic systems, will be affected accordingly.

(c) The Cerebellum Theory

Cerebellum is a section of the brain located at the lower back of the brain. Many researchers believe that the cerebellum plays an important role in helping to process language. The cerebellum theory, also called automaticity theory, states that dyslexia is caused by physical differences in the cerebellum. The cerebellum is also responsible for coordination and one's ability to estimate how much time has passed. This may explain why many people with dyslexia have problems with both coordination and time management. Here the biological claim is that the dyslexic's cerebellum is mildly dysfunctional and that a number of cognitive difficulties ensue because of that. Firstly, the cerebellum plays a role in motor control and therefore in speech articulation. It is postulated that retarded or dysfunctional articulation would lead to deficient phonological representations. Secondly, the cerebellum plays a role in the automatization of overlearned tasks, such as driving, typing and reading. A weak capacity to automatize would affect, among other things, the learning of grapheme—phoneme correspondences. Support for the cerebellar theory comes from evidence of poor performance of dyslexics in a large number of motor tasks, in dual tasks demonstrating impaired automatization of balance, and in time estimation, a non-motor cerebellar task. Brain imaging studies have also shown anatomical, metabolic and activation differences in the cerebellum of dyslexics

(d) The Magnocellular Theory

The magnocellular theory argues that dyslexia is caused by the impaired development of large brain cells (neurons) known as magnocells. Magnocells are responsible for making sure that your eyes look at the right words at the right time when you are reading. Defects with the magnocells may cause someone with dyslexia to look at letters and words in the wrong order and at the wrong time. This may explain why many people with the condition say that words on a page often appear fuzzy and out of focus.

The magnocellular theory postulates that the magnocellular dysfunction is not restricted to the visual pathways but is generalized to all modalities (visual and auditory as well as tactile). Furthermore, as the cerebellum receives massive input from various magnocellular systems in the brain, it is also predicted to be affected by the general magnocellular defect (Stein *et al.*, 2001). Through a single biological cause, this theory therefore manages to account for all known manifestations of dyslexia: visual, auditory, tactile, motor and, consequently, phonological. Evidence specifically relevant to the magnocellular theory includes magnocellular abnormalities in the medial as well as the lateral geniculate nucleus of dyslexics' brains, poor performance of dyslexics in the tactile domain, and the co-occurrence of visual and auditory problems in certain dyslexics.

(e) Working Memory Theory

The brain first keeps all new information in a part of the memory, called the 'working memory'. The information is then either transferred to your long-term memory or forgotten. If transferred to long-term memory, the information is retained in the memory and is available for recall whenever needed. Otherwise, the information is lost and is not available for subsequent use. For example, if a person is able to remember the year of his birth, it is because the working memory in his brain has moved that information into the long-term memory. However, it is unlikely that he will remember the registration number of his neighbour's car, even though he sees it every day. That is because the working memory knows that the information is of little use so it and discards it. Dyslexia is the result of the brain discarding new information relating to reading and writing instead of transferring it to the long-term memory.

(f) The Rapid Auditory Processing Theory

The rapid auditory processing theory is an alternative to the phonological deficit theory. This theory specifies that the primary deficit lies in the perception of short or rapidly varying sounds. Support for this theory arises from evidence that dyslexics show poor performance on a number of auditory tasks, including frequency discrimination and temporal order judgment. Backward masking tasks, in particular, demonstrate a 100-fold (40 dB) difference in sensitivity between normals and dyslexics. Abnormal neurophysiological responses to various auditory stimuli have also been demonstrated. The failure to correctly represent short sounds and fast transitions would cause further difficulties in particular when such acoustic events are the cues to phonemic contrasts, as in /ba/ versus /da/. There is also evidence that dyslexics may have poorer categorical perception of certain contrasts.

(g) The Visual Theory

The visual theory (Lovegrove *et al.*, 1980; Livingstone *et al.*, 1991; Stein and Walsh, 1997) reflects another long standing tradition in the study of dyslexia, that of considering it as a visual impairment giving rise to difficulties with the processing of letters and words on a page of text. This may take the form of unstable binocular fixations, poor vergence, or increased visual crowding. The visual theory does not exclude a phonological deficit, but emphasizes a visual contribution to reading problems, at least in some dyslexic individuals. At the biological level, the proposed etiology of the visual dysfunction is based on the division of the visual system into two distinct pathways that have different roles and properties: the magnocellular and parvocellular pathways. The theory postulates that the magnocellular pathway is selectively disrupted in certain dyslexic individuals, leading to deficiencies in visual processing, and, via the posterior parietal cortex, to abnormal binocular control and visuospatial attention. Evidence for magnocellular dysfunction comes from anatomical studies showing abnormalities of the magnocellular layers of the lateral geniculate nucleus (Livingstone *et al.*, 1991), psychophysical studies showing decreased sensitivity in the magnocellular range, i.e. low spatial frequencies and high temporal frequencies in dyslexics, and brain imaging studies.

(h) Perceptual Visual—Noise Exclusion Hypothesis

The concept of a perceptual noise exclusion (Visual—Noise) deficit is an emerging hypothesis, supported by research showing that dyslexic subjects experience difficulty in performing visual tasks such as motion detection in the presence of perceptual distractions, but do not show the same impairment when the distracting factors are removed in an experimental setting. The researchers have analogized their findings concerning visual discrimination tasks to findings in other research related to auditory discrimination tasks. They assert that dyslexic symptoms arise because of an impaired ability to filter out both visual and auditory distractions, and to categorize information so as to distinguish the important sensory data from the irrelevant.

New researches are still going on which generate new theories and data leading to have better indepth knowledge about learning disabilities. Such innovations help in diagnosis and interventions.

Identification and Diagnosis of Learning Disabilities

It is not easy to detect learning disabilities, specially as they can go undetected in the early stages of childhood and even at the stage of schooling. Parents may feel that their child is a late learner and ignore the fact that he is not able to read or write or sometimes they may think that the child is not concentrating on studies. Many parents scold the child for not learning. In school also teachers are unaware of the difficulties of the child and punish him. They also complain about the child to his parents. The child becomes anxious and feels frustrated with his difficulty in learning to read or write. He may develop behavioural problems like aggression, hyperactivity etc. In such circumstances the fact that learning disabilities of the child are the cause is totally ignored and parents and teachers focus upon his bahavioural problems. Gradually the child develops low self-esteem and low self—confidence. He may not like to come to the school. Identification, diagnosis and treatment of the difficulty is extremely important before the child becomes totally de-motivated.

Learning disabilities are usually diagnosed during the elementary school stage. In some cases, the child is diagnosed as having the problem when he grows older and finds it difficult to learn grammar and syntax and to read longer and more complex material. Stuttering or cluttering is also sometimes related to learning disabilities.

The services of a professional are required to identify such disabilities. A teacher may detect some signs and refer to a psychologist or other health professional to ascertain if the child is suffering from any disorder. The following symptoms can be noted to refer the child for professional help:

- Difficulty characterized by letter and number reversals are most common. Other children can have these difficulties also but generally children overcome such difficulties by the time they cross the age of 7 or 8. Those who are not able to are a matter of concern.

- Difficulty in pronouncing long words.
- Learning the alphabet, days of the weeks, colours, shapes, and numbers
- Learning to read and write his or her name
- Difficulty copying from the board or a book can also suggest problems.
- Handwriting and fine-motor coordination
- There may be a general disorganization of written work. A child may not be able to remember content, even if it involves a favorite video or storybook.
- Problems with spatial relationships can extend beyond the classroom and be observed on the playground. The child may appear to be uncoordinated and have difficulty with organized sports or games.
- Difficulty with left and right is common, and often dominance for either hand has not been established.
- In the early grades, music and dance are often used to enhance academic learning. Children with dyslexia can have difficulty moving to the rhythm of the music.
- A child may have difficulty remembering or understanding what he hears.
- Recalling sequences of things or more than one command at a time can be difficult.
- Parts of words or parts of whole sentences may be missed, and words can come out sounding funny. The wrong word or a similar word may be used instead.
- Children struggling with this problem may know what they want to say but have trouble finding the actual words to express their thoughts.
- Children may become withdrawn and appear to be depressed. They may begin to act out, drawing attention away from their learning difficulty.
- Problems with self-esteem can arise, and peer and sibling interactions can become strained.
- These children may lose their interest in school—related activities and appear to be unmotivated or lazy.
- The emotional symptoms and signs are just as important as the academic and require equal attention.

Even when the children grow, the above symptoms could remain. Besides, they may:

- Display abilities to read and spell far below the people of their age.
- Avoid reading and writing
- Work slowly on reading and writing assignments and tests
- Not be able to learn a foreign language

Davis, 1992) identified 37 common characteristics of dyslexics only by which they can be identified. Most of these are common to other forms of learning diabilities discussed earlier. Summary of the characteristics by which such children could be identified is given below:

1. They are bright, highly intelligent and articulate but are unable to read, write or spell.
2. They are said, "not trying hard enough",
3. They can be helped in the school setting.
4. They test well orally.
5. Dyslexics have low poor self-esteem; easily frustrated and emotional about school work.
6. Talented in art, drama, music, sports, mechanics, story-telling, sales, business, etc.
7. They appear to daydream and do not have concept of time.
8. Difficulty sustaining attention; seems hyper-active
9. They can learn better with hands—on experience, demonstrations, experimentation, observation, and visual aids.
10. They feel dizziness, headaches, or stomachaches while reading.
11. They feel confused by letters, numbers, words, etc.
12. They repeat words and sentences while reading or writing; make additions or omissions on their own.
13. Complains non-existent movement while reading, writing or copying.
14. They may have difficulty with vision without any problem of the eyes.
15. Extremely observant, or lacks depth perception and peripheral vision.

16. Try to read again and again with little comprehension.
17. Spell phonetically and inconsistently.
18. They hear voices that are not there and are easily distracted by sounds.
19. Difficulty putting thoughts into words; speaks in halting phrases; stutters under stress
20. Trouble with writing or copying; find it difficult to hold pencil or pen; handwriting is illegible.
21. Poor coordination, difficulties with fine motor skills and tasks.
22. Can be confused with left/right, over/under.
23. Has difficulty in telling and managing time,
24. Dependency on finger counting and other tricks; knows answers, but can't do it on paper.
25. Difficulty in counting objects and dealing with money.
26. Can do arithmetic, but fails word problems, cannot grasp algebra or higher math.
27. Excellent long-term memory for experiences, locations and faces.
28. Poor memory for sequences, facts, and information that has not been experienced.
29. Thinks primarily with images and feelings, not sounds or words
30. Disordered.
31. Can be a troublemaker, or too quiet.
32. Had unusually early or late developmental stages (talking, crawling, walking, tying shoelaces).
33. Prone to ear infections, sensitive to foods.
34. Can have sleep disorder; can do bedwetting beyond appropriate age.
35. Tolerance for pain is either very high or very low.
36. Strong sense of justice; emotional and sensitive.
37. Mistakes and symptoms increase dramatically with confusion, time pressure, emotional stress, or poor health.

Identification of learning disability is directly related to the development of the child. After the birth, there are specific times that are known as milestones in the development of a child. For example, after the birth, the child cries, if one does not, it is a matter of concern for the doctors. Similarly, family members watch the child whether he gets attracted towards sounds, lights, objects and so on. Parents watch for the child to utter the word or take a step at the proper age in his life. Delays in these activities must be noticed at the home and later in the school if the child does not show achievements in learning at par with other children. It is to be mentioned here that some children take a little more time than others in speaking, walking or learning. This could be normal. In such cases help of a professional must be taken. The reasons of delay could be different from learning disabilities. There is a possibility that the child got ill for a long duration or has visual problems or some family stress. Those possibilities should be taken care of before the child is reported as learning disabled.

HOW TO RECOGNISE A LEARNING DISABLED

Indications at Pre-School

Before the child is sent to school, parents and other family members should observe their child's behaviour. He could be restless with short attention span. He may not be able to concentrate on one object or thing for longer time. At younger age children learn nursery rhymes, but a learning disabled child may not be able to remember the rhymes or a few words in the rhyme that have similarity such as hat and bat, ball and tall while playing they may not understand directions like right or left or up and down. They may also lack in hand-feet coordination and other abilities relating to physical exercises. They may find it difficult in catching a ball.

Indications at Elementary School Level

When the child is sent to school, he should be observed for his extent of learning. Learning disabled children may like to listen to stories but avoid reading. They may also take longer time in completing the assignments than other children of their class. They find it difficult to put things in a specified sequence and do the simple mathematical calculations by putting small beads with them. They also need help in dressing up, combing their hairs or tying shoe laces.

Indications at Secondary School Levels

The handwriting of learning disabled is irregular. Words are illegible and spellings are incorrect. Such children cannot reproduce numbers, take notes in the class very slow, copy from the chalkboard in a long time and get poor grades. In case the problems are not identified at a young age and taken care of, they could persist and become more pronounced as the children grow.

DIAGNOSIS OF LEARNING DISABILITIES

It is very difficult to diagnose learning disabilities. Early identification on the basis of the above mentioned behaviours can help in diagnosing the problem and the child can be referred to the concerned specialist for appropriate tests. There are a number of tests that can be helpful in determining the functional level of the child. These tests are intelligence tests, the auditory tests, the visual tests and kinesthetic tests. The tests also find out how all the sensory systems work in coordination with each other.

There are two stages in diagnosing the learning disability:

- screening, and
- assessment

A general screening is possible with observations by the parents and other family members or friends. Teachers can also identify the general behaviour which is different with those of others in the class. Simple activities can also be planned to see if the child is facing problems with learning. This screening can help in identifying the child for further diagnosis and assessment which would require the help of professionals.

The tests that are used to diagnose learning disability are standardized tests and can provide good results. Most of the tests used involve games or puzzles which a child enjoys doing. He does not get a feeling that he is put on some test. He should be made comfortable before he is given a test. Parents can help the child in getting mentally prepared for the tests. If the testing is done in a school setting, the teacher can help the child by talking about the person who will be with the child. With young children, the psychologist may visit the child's classroom before the testing so that the child is familiar with him.

Some of the tests that can be used for diagnosis of learning problems are as below (The list is only indicative):

1. Wechsler Intelligence Scale for Children—Third Edition (WISC-III)
2. Kaufman Assessment Battery for Children (KABC)
3. Stanford—Binet Intelligence Scale
4. Woodcock—Johnson Psycho—Educational Battery
5. Peabody Individual Achievement Tests—Revised (PIAT)
6. Wechsler Individual Achievement Tests (WIAT)
7. Kaufman Tests of Educational Achievement (KTEA)
8. Bender Gestalt Test of Visual Motor Perception
9. Beery Developmental Test of Visual-Motor Integration
10. Motor—Free Visual Perception Test
11. Visual Aural Digit Span Test (VADS)
12. Test of Auditory Perception (TAPS)
13. Test of Visual Perception (TVPS)
14. Peabody Picture Vocabulary Test-Revised
15. Expressive One—Word Picture Vocabulary Test
16. Test for Auditory Comprehension of Language
17. Bhatia Battery
18. Woodcock Reading Mastery Test
19. Woodcock—Johnson Psychological Battery
20. Weschler Individual Achievement Test
21. The Decoding Skills Test
22. The Kaufman Test of Educational Achievement
23. Lindamood Auditory conceptualization Test
24. Test of Phonological Skills (Linguisystems)
25. Woodcock Reading Mastery Test
26. Informal Reading Inventory
27. Weschsler Individual Achievement Test
28. Qualitative Inventory of Spelling Development
29. Clinical Evaluation of Language Fundamentals
30. Woodcock—Johnson Test of Cognitive Abilities
31. Bender Gestalt Test
32. Visual Motor Integration Test
33. Rey Complex Figure Drawing
34. Slingerland Screening Test

Details of Some Tests that are frequently used:—

Name of the Tests	*Measures the following*
Comprehensive Test of Phonological Processing (CTOPP), by Richard K. Wagner, Joseph K. Torgesen, and Carol A. Rashotte, 1999	Tests 3 skills: phonological awareness, phonological memory, and rapid naming. Subtests for 5 & 6 year olds include phoneme elision, word blending, and matching the first and last sounds in a word. Also tests rapid naming of colours and objects, and memory for a string of digits and non-word sounds.
Dynamic Indicators of Basic Early Literacy Skills (5th Ed.), edited by Roland H. Good III and Ruth A. Kaminski, University of Oregon	K-3 Assessment tools.
Fox in a Box, Marilyn Adams, (1999)	Assessment and intervention kit. Phonemic awareness, phonics, reading/oral expressiveness, and listening/writing expressiveness.
Phonological Awareness Literacy Screening (PALS), created through the Virginia Early Intervention Reading Initiative	Faculty from the Univ. of Virginia's Curry School of Education created this assessment tool, which is available for a nominal per student fee by those outside of Virginia. Individual children's scores are tabulated, with links to the activities on the website that support any student deficits.
The Phonological Awareness Test Robertson & Salter, 1995	Contains 5 measures of phonemic awareness, including segmentation, isolation, deletion, substitution, and blending.
Test of Phonological Awareness (TOPA), Joseph K. Torgesen, Brian R. Bryant, 1994	Kindergarten and Early Elementary versions. In the Kindergarten versions the student identifies which of 3 words begins with the same sound as a stimulus word. Also which of 3 words has a different initial sound than a stimulus word.
Test of Word Reading Efficiency (TOWRE), Joseph K. Torgesen, Richard K Wagner, and Carol A. Rashotte, 1999	Test used for first graders and above. There are 2 subtests. One measures the child's ability to read sight words, and the other is a test of phonemic decoding of nonwords.
The Texas Primary Reading Inventory (K-2)	Kit includes a teacher's guide, an intervention activities guide, magnetic board and set of magnetic letters, laminated story cards, and 26 student record sheets for a K, 1, & 2 classroom.
The Yopp-Singer Test of Phoneme Segmentation, Haley Yopp, 1995	This is a brief test that can be used for kindergarten students. The 22 items ask the child to pronounce a phoneme in a word that varies from 1-3 phonemes in length.

Use of tests and diagnosis would depend upon the type of learning disability. If the child has difficulty in speaking, the service of a speech therapist would be needed to give an appropriate test. The academic achievements or mathematical problems can be diagnosed using standardized tests and in this case services of a psychologist are needed. Intelligence and commensurate achievement is one criteria of diagnosis.

Another criteria of diagnosis is response to intervention (RTI). Under this technique all the children are screened, those with difficulty (who can not achieve through classroom instruction known as Tier I instructions) are identified. Tier II intervention is provided to such students with remedial classes or special education services. Tier III intervention is also included in RTI programme to provide specific teachings and see the response of the child. If the child still has difficulty in learning, he is diagnosed as learning-disabled child. In developed countries this model is popular in diagnosing learning disabled children.

Assessment through various standardized tests as indicated above is helpful in preparing an intervention plan after the learning disabled child is identified and also tackle his behavioural problems if any. The tests provide an account of child's level of skill in comparison to the skill that is considered as normal for the child of his age. For finalizing the test results it is necessary that other therapists observe the child also as there could be a learning problem due to for example ear infection. In articulatory problems the doctor should rule out the child for any problem with the vocal cord or throat. If the child has difficulty in writing from the chalkboard, it should be ensured that he does not have a vision problem or there is proper lighting in the room. In other words, before the child is labeled as having learning disability, the other factors that could hamper the child's learning should be taken into account.

It must also be noted here that each and every child has some or the other innate skill even if he has learning problems. Some children are gifted with music sense; some are good in painting or other fine arts. It is necessary to identify the special skill in the learning disabled child so as to nurture his/her skill. It has to be understood by parents and teachers that it is not necessary that each child must be excellent in mathematics or science or language and so on. Family and school should help the child in developing himself with the skills one possesses. In developed countries this has been accepted while it is yet to be recognized by the people in developing countries like India. Parents find it very hard to accept the truth. Greater awareness can help in dealing with the situation. There are examples of learning disabled who have excelled in life far more than the normal learners.

To sum up following experts can help in diagnosis and identification of a disabled child:

1. School Counsellor
2. Teachers
3. Psychologist
4. Neuropsychologist
5. Psychometrist
6. Occupational therapist
7. Speech and language therapist.

It is not necessary that each and every child with learning disability has to contact all the above listed experts. A learning disabled child can be diagnosed/ identified by any one of them depending upon the child's problems. In some cases a team of experts is needed to diagnose the difficulties of the child.

Causes of Learning Disability

A number of researches have been conducted to find out the causes of learning disabilities. These are yet to be explained completely and with authenticity. It has been seen that sometimes there is no cause but a learning disability exists. Some of the factors that have been identified with learning disabilities are:

1. GENETIC FACTORS

Researches show that learning disability is genetically inherited. It is widely accepted that a dyslexic's brain cells are arranged differently or function differently as compared to the normal person's brain. These brain cell abnormalities are produced by genetic factors. About 85 per cent of dyslexics have immediate relatives with the same disorders. It has been found out that genes carried on the X chromosome play an important role in generating this problem. A number of genes have been identified that cause learning disability. It has been noticed that learning disabilities pass on from one generation to the other. Researches have also revealed that the problem is more common in males than females. It has been identified as neurological impairment.

Other researches show that it is not necessary that if somebody is suffering in the family from a specific type of learning disability, the child will suffer from the same. For example, if the parent has speech disorder the child may have writing disorder. Therefore, it is not established that one specific learning disorder is due to the disorder in the family directly.

There is another view on the theory of transferring of family disorder to the child and this attributes the transfer to social rather than genetic factors. It is believed that each and every family has some learning environment. A good learning environment facilitates the child learning. There is a possibility that where parents are not good in expression or language or are not much talkative they may not interact with the child much which may hamper the child's development. He may not acquire speaking skills or expressions and may be termed as learning disabled.

2. DEFECTS IN BRAIN STRUCTURE

The brain of the child develops during the total pregnancy period. As the foetus grows, the brain develops as a complex organ of the body interconnecting various neurons. This period is very vulnerable and any small disruption in the development may lead to brain dysfunction. If such disruption takes place in the initial stages of fetal development, the child may have mental retardation or the fetus may not survive, but when the cells become stronger in the later stages of pregnancy, the movement of cells from one place to another may have some errors in interconnections. It has been seen that these errors may lead to defective brain structure and various forms of learning disabilities may occur.

3. USE OF DRUGS

Use of drugs by the parents is harmful to the development of children. This harm is done in various ways. Firstly, if the mother is in the habit of smoking or taking alcohol this may affect the development of the brain of the fetus during pregnancy period. Sometimes during pregnancy, mothers develop a number of complications and remain on various drugs. The effect of these drugs directly goes to the fetus which may damage the child. It has also been seen through researches that alcohol affects the development of brain in the fetus negatively. It hampers the development of neurons. Similar is the case with smoking. The child may look like the normal babies but in fact he may be of lesser weight which makes him vulnerable to learning disabilities. The drug users also have a negative impact on the brain development. It damages the brain receptors. The physical response to the environment may be hampered due to damage of receptors. Precautions are therefore, necessary during pregenancy. Also during delivery if the oxygen is cut off to the fetus, it can impair brain activities and as a result learning disabilities may occur.

4. ENVIRONMENT

After the child is born, the brain cells and network continues to develop at least for a year. During this period if there is any disruption, the child may develop learning disabilities. Scientists have experimented on toxics that are a part of the environment. Cadmium and lead are two such toxics. The scientists are carrying on experiments to see their impact on the functioning of the brain. The experiments on animals show that exposure to lead caused changes in the brain resulting in the pace of learning. Environment in modern days is polluted due to excessive use of pesticides for agriculture production. The pesticides also damage the functions of the brain.

5. ILLNESS OR INJURY

Learning disabilities can also take place if there is any injury to the brain due to some accident or illness. For example, if the child is exposed to radiation in the early stages of life, it can affect the brain function. This could be due to tumor in the brain. Newly born may also suffer from certain illnesses which also affect brain development negatively. Children suffering from asthma or diabetes or cancer could also have learning disabilities. Poor nutrition has negative impact on the development of brain

6. PHONEMIC KNOWLEDGE

Phonemic specially relates to the knowledge of phonemes. The lack of knowledge of phonemic leads to problems in spoken language. Such children are not able to connect sounds with spoken alphabets or words. There are various tasks involved in speaking a language. These tasks are given in the Table 1.

If the child is unable to do any of the tasks of the spoken language and is not aware of the above phonemics, he will have problems in learning inter-connectivity among alphabets and sounds. This problem especially relates to dyslexia. Brain has long-term memory and combines and matches the words on its own and, thus, the speech takes place. Any dysfunction of the brain may create problem in this task.

Table 1

Phoneme Segmentation	*Deletion*	*Matching*	*Counting*	*Substitution*	*Blending*	*Rhyming*
In segmentation child is required to recognize the sounds of various spoken alphabets. For example, what the sound child hears in 'hot' or the last sound of 'hot.'	The child has to recognize various words if certain sounds are deleted from the words. For example, in the hat word child should be able to recognize the sound if the sound of /h/ is deleted.	In matching the child has to see whether words starting with the same alphabets have similar sound. For example, cat, cute, care or bat, bite, better	In counting the child has to recognize more than one sound of a word. For example, he has to notice the sounds in the word dog or caught. In this he has to recognize more than one sound.	In substitution the child has to see that if one alphabet is replaced how the word would change in another word. For example, in rat if /r/ is replaced by /s/ what word would it produce.	Blending involves putting various sounds together of different alphabets. For example, pot or milk	Rhyming involves connecting one word with other words of the same rhyme. For example, `rat'. The other words of rhyme of rat are sat, cat, pat, hat etc.

7. DISADVANTAGED GROUPS

The persons who have no or little exposure to the outside world may develop learning disability. These disadvantaged groups are people living in remote and backward areas, economically backward or technologically backward etc. There are children who have never seen any school or books, they have never been to the city. There are tribes who are unaware of clothes, foods etc. Children from such families have total lack of awareness about what is happening in the world. Such situation can create learning problems among the children. Emotionally deprived children can also develop learning problems.

Impact of Learning Disabilities on Children

Learning disabilities affect the development of personalities in a negative manner. People with such disabilities feel that they are different from others and, therefore, they would not be accepted by the society. This keeps them aloof from others and makes them feel lonely. Some specific effects of learning disabilities on persons affected have been discussed here.

LOW SELF-ESTEEM

A child with learning disabilities who sees his friends and other students reading and writing well develops low self-esteem, as he does not understand as to why he is not able to be like them. According to Erik Erikson, every child must resolve the conflicts between a positive self-image and feelings of inferiority during the very early years of school. Positive self-image takes place when the child sees that he is getting recognized, his efforts are fruitful and he is successful. If children succeed in school, they will develop positive feelings about themselves. If children meet failure they feel that they are inferior to others. Researches show that instead of developing a feeling of being productive, they come to the conclusion that their environment controls them. They feel incompetent. Research also brings out that the feelings of inferiority develop by the age of ten. After this age, it becomes extremely difficult to help the child develop a positive self-image. This is a powerful argument for early intervention.

AVOIDANCE

Children with learning disabilities develop avoidance behaviours and try not to be in situations where they are supposed to read or write. They may not attend classes or may pose as sick in the class to avoid reading. As a result, they end up in losing their learning and fall behind more and more. They do not like the school or tuitions in case their problem is not identified and remedial measures taken. Other students of the class may make fun of them when they are not able to read or write or if their handwriting is not good. Many learning disabled, eventually, come to the conclusion that they want to leave school.

AGGRESSION

Children with learning disabilities are not able to cope up with the studies and, as a result, feel very depressed and irritable. They develop aggressive behaviours and anxiety. If they do not get support from the parents, peers and teachers they may develop withdrawal symptoms. Social scientists have frequently observed that frustration produces anger. This can be clearly seen in many dyslexics. The anger is targeted towards school, studies and teachers. Parents also face the anger of learning disabled child. His anger can be controlled in the company of the persons with whom he feels comfortable and can share his problems or in the environment where he feels secure. Sometimes, in such protected atmosphere, these children cry to give vent to their frustrating experiences. The tension between the expectation of independence and the child's acquired dependence causes great internal conflicts. The adolescent dyslexic uses his anger to break away from those people on whom he feels so dependent. Because of these factors, it may be difficult for parents to help their teenage dyslexic. It is necessary that learning disabled children have a strong support system within the family and outside.

LACK OF SUPPORT SYSTEM

The child with learning disabilities loses his support system in the school, as fellow students, due to ignorance, feel that the child is stupid or mentally retarded. The friends try to avoid the company of such a child. Thus, these children are left to themselves. Teachers, if not aware of the problem, accuse learning disabled children as lazy or naughty, not interested in studies etc. and punish them for not learning. Many a time, parents are also not supportive and compare their child with other children of his age. Such a situation leaves no support for the child and he feels totally alone and neglected.

THEIR OWN WORLD

Such learning disabled children without adequate support systems create their own world of fantasies and fun, which may not be acceptable to the society. They brood and think. Their thoughts are so different from others that they feel totally unfit in the society. They have their own creative answers to the problems or questions asked which do not match with those of text books. Teachers as well as parents scold them.

FEAR OF FAILURE

Children with learning disabilities always suffer from 'failure syndrome'. They are afraid of being criticized by others in the class as well as outside school. They feel that they would not be accepted by their fellow beings. They fear that they would not get good grades. They develop a feeling that classmates would laugh at them if they are not able to read and write like them. Since such children usually have illegible handwriting also, they feel ashamed. Gradually they develop 'learned helplessness'.

EMOTIONAL PROBLEMS

Orton was one of the first researchers to describe the emotional aspects of dyslexia. According to his research, dyslexics are generally happy and well adjusted. Their emotional problems begin when they start reading and instructions provided to them do not match their learning style. The emotional problems of children with dyslexia are due to their inability to meet expectations of the parents, teachers and friends. Time and again, dyslexics have to face the comments like "He's such a bright child; if only he would try harder." They feel that they make silly mistakes and develop problems in maintaining social relationships. Anxiety is the most frequent emotional symptom for the dyslexic child. Dyslexics become fearful because of their constant frustration and confusion in school. They anticipate failures and avoid school-related situations. This is true in case of other learning disabled children also.

DEPRESSION

Depression is also a frequent complication among the learning disabled. It is not necessary that all the learning disabled develop depression. But these children suffer from intense feelings of sorrow, despair and gloom. When they are not able to show their anger outwardly, they direct it towards self. This inward anger makes them depressed. They may not show their feelings of depression but internally they remain very sad and with this masked depression, they may develop as depressed adult.

FAMILY PROBLEMS

Like any handicapping condition, learning disability has an impact on the child's family. The family members sometimes try to hide the fact that they have a learning disabled child at home. For this purpose, they avoid meeting neighbors or do not allow the child to go out and play with other children. Families with such children also suffer with sibling rivalry. The learning disabled child gets the most of the parents' attention, time, and resources, and, therefore, the other children in the family may feel neglected. Specific developmental dyslexia runs in families as discussed elsewhere. When faced with a child who is having school problems, parents may react by denying the existence of such a problem and believe that the child is normal and would achieve. In certain cases, the parents may relive their own failures and frustrations through their child's school experience. This emotional outbreak interferes with the adult's parenting skills.

Specific Needs of Learning Disabled

EMOTIONAL ADJUSTMENT

Learning disabled children are often not dealt with care and concern and, therefore, encounter emotional adjustment problems. They find it difficult to make friends and are maladjusted in making relationships and so they feel very lonely. In due course, they may develop symptoms of withdrawal and anxiety. Their insecurities are reflected in their physical behaviours also. They may start biting their nails, show aggression and indulge in mannerisms for getting attention from others. They can be impulsive and irritable. This non-adjustment may lead to lack of concentration in their studies. They are restless and not able to adjust with environmental difficulties because of their emotional hang-ups. Emotional adjustment problems of the disabled may lead to development of low self-esteem and low levels of self-confidence. It is therefore extremely essential that such children are provided emotional security which is possible only when they are loved.

DEPENDENCE AND LACK OF SECURITY

Disabled children feel themselves dependent on others if they are not made aware of their disabilities and coping strategies. However, this depends upon the type of disability and its degree. If a learning disabled child also has some other disability such as vision problem or hearing problem, the child, most of the times, remains dependent on others. Parents also, because of lack of confidence in the child's ability, do not give enough freedom to the child to become independent. This generates insecurity in the child and he remains dependent even when he grows up. Parents should provide the protection as per need. Learning disabled children have to be independent.

ADJUSTMENT WITH THE ENVIRONMENT

The disabled children are non-adjusted towards their environment in two ways. On the one hand, the structures and buildings of the schools as well as house and other places are not generally disabled friendly and on the other, the attitudes of the peer group and the other people of the society are not favourable towards them. If the school structure does not have any ramp for moving the wheel chairs, the facility of Braille system for the blind children, availability of hearing aids etc., it becomes difficult for the children with various kinds of disabilities to adjust with the environment. Schools or the houses, which have multi-storey buildings and do not have disabled friendly lifts, create problems for the children with disabilities. Even if the lifts are available, signs are not available in the Braille system and if there is no announcement system, it is difficult for blind children to reach to the desired floor. Learning disabled children generally do not have these problems. But if they have any of the other disability along with their learning disability the above problems emerge. Generally learning disabled are the laughing stocks for the others. The environment surrounding the learning disabled children must be disability sensitive.

The attitudes of the people towards disabilities are generally unfavorable. 'You cannot do' is the common phrase used for disabled children. Sometimes, because of curiosity and lack of awareness, the children in the peer group ask undesirable questions from the children with disabilities, which make the latter feel embarrassed and neglected. It has been observed that teachers also make undesirable remarks about such children. Teachers do not encourage the disabled children to participate in the curricular activities and in other group activities. Such attitudes leave a feeling of neglect among the children with disabilities.

It is also a common phenomenon that in families in which there is a disabled child, parents avoid taking him or her along with them on outings or on family visits. There have been cases when families with a learning disabled child do not disclose that they have such a child. They sometime do not even count him or her in the number of children they have. Such situations create obstacles in the development of children with disabilities to become self-dependent and lead a normal life. Community has to be sensitive towards the needs of the learning disabled.

FEELING OF GUILT

A disabled child, when constantly reminded about his disability in the school and in the family, develops a feeling of guilt, which hampers his normal adjustment with the society. Teachers scold the child if he is not able to perform the mathematical problems. He may give strange answers to the language questions in the class. He may not read the paragraph in the manner others can do and thus attract laughter from others. This gradually gives him a feeling of guilt. He avoids doing things in front of others or may be truant. Instead of reminding such children about what they cannot do, their specific abilities must be identified and nurtured to take them out of the sense of inferiority and guilt.

LACK OF AWARENESS ABOUT DISABILITIES

Disabled children face a lot of problems in making adjustments due to lack of awareness in the society about various disabilities. Parents are ignorant about how to deal with a disabled child. They sometimes do not know what facilities are available for their disabled child and how to avail of them. In the case of the learning disabled this problem is more acute as its identification is difficult. It is relatively easy to identify a child with hearing problem or visual problem. It may take a longer time to identify the learning disabled as generally the parents as well as teachers think that the child is not paying much attention towards the studies. Since the recognition of learning disabilities in India is a relatively recent phenomenon, there is a lack of awareness about its symptoms as well as coping strategies. There is a need to organize awareness programmes at school as well as community level to generate awareness about learning disabilities and needs of such children.

Educational Problems of Learning Disabled Children

Learning disability is a hidden problem which is not easy to detect. School children suffer with several types of learning difficulties. Symptoms are not common. Some children exhibit problems with speaking or hearing correctly and some have problems relating to spelling words, speaking or hand-writing and others relating to language, movement, etc. These problems are discussed in some detail below:

PROBLEMS RELATING TO SPEECH AND HEARING

1. *Difficulty in learning certain phrases*: Anush was in Class IV but it was difficult for him to understand the directions correctly. During physical education lessons he used to get confused when he was asked to take a turn to left or right. Kishan, a child of Class III was asked by the teacher to read a paragraph after a certain line on a certain page. He could not locate which para he was supposed to read till he was helped by the fellow students. Learning disabled children do not understand phrases like "Read sentence before or after this' or 'turn to your left or right'. They find it difficult to speak as the other normal students of the class or the children of their age do. While speaking they use incorrect grammar. They know very few words and therefore their vocabulary is very limited. They are not able to speak complete words. They drop some of the words while speaking. Their communication is also not in order as they find it difficult in sequencing the conversation in a logical order. Sometimes they speak without any focus on what they are saying. In case a long paragraph is to be read they forget what was read to them. Sometimes they remember only those points which are not relevant in the speech. It is difficult for them to speak

long words or long sentences. They make pauses while speaking and are able to express themselves only with great difficulty.

2. *Difficulty in learning alphabets:* Geetika happily shifted from play school to nursery. At this time, she was taught reading and writing alphabets. While other children of her age could learn recognising the alphabets she was finding it very difficult to recognize the sounds of each alphabet and how these were different from one another. Gradually she could learn some alphabets but her handwriting was extremely poor. Moreover she could never learn to differentiate among alphabets that used to look alike such as 'p' and 'q' or 'b' and'd'.
3. *Retrieval, reversal and recall:* Dyslexic children find difficulty with word retrieval, naming objects or recalling names. It is also problematic for them to count the numbers in reverse order. For example, while the child can count numbers from one to ten, he cannot do so from ten to one.
4. *Phonological awareness:* Vikalp was asked in the class to count the letters in the word 'animal'. He tried a number of times but failed. He was mixing the letters and could not count the alphabets in words. The dyslexic children also find it difficult to count and recognize syllables in words. Such children are unable to produce rhymes in the words.
5. *Phonemic awareness:* Dyslexic children do not have clear phonemic awareness. Phonemic awareness relates to difficulty with hearing and manipulating sounds in words. Spoken words are formed by discrete phonemes. For example, the word CAT comes from the sounds [k], [æ], and [t]). As a result, affected individuals have difficulty associating these sounds with the visual letters that make up written words.
6. *Auditary discrimination:* Auditary discrimination is also difficult for dyslexic children. This may relate to auditary processing disorder under which a child cannot distinguish different sounds in words. He may feel all sounds as noise and cannot relate the sounds with words. That is also one of the reasons why such children suffer with speech disorder at later stages in life.

7. *Word meanings:* The affected children are unable to associate individual words with their correct meanings.
8. *Concept of time:* Children suffering with learning disabilities may not have concept of time. They may not understand 6 a.m. and 6 p.m. and so on. If left on their own, they reach the school late. They cannot schedule their activities according to time. During examinations they need extra time to complete the work. They cannot plan their activities according to the availability of time. They cannot understand the date and time through calendars or watch. They also do not have the concept of weeks, months, etc. They do not understand the unit of time like seconds, hour or minute.
9. *Combination of words*: There could be confusion among learning disabled children in joining various words or understanding different combinations of words. The child who reads very slowly and hesitantly, who reads without fluency word by word, or who constantly loses his place in the text, thereby leaving out whole chunks of text or reading the same passage twice, has a reading problem.

PROBLEMS RELATING TO LANGUAGE

- *Spellings:* Due to difficulty in understanding, and the combination of words and sounds together, children with dyslexia make mistakes in spelling the words correctly. Generally they omit the vowels.

any ('eny')
many ('meny')
does ('dus')
said ('sed')
they ('thay')
because ('becos')
island ('iland')
eyes ('ies')
friend ('frend')
enough ('enuff')

- *Order of alphabets in a word:* Dyslexics may reverse the order of two letters especially when the word has similarity with some other word. For example, the child may not be able to write the word 'dose' correctly as it is similar to the word 'does'. 'Mirror writing', i.e., writing letters as they appear in a mirror, is not at all unusual for dyslexics.
- *Words without phonetic spellings:* Dyslexics misspell words whose spellings are not phonetic. They may write 'shud' for 'should' or 'mite' for 'might'. Dyslexic individuals also have difficulty distinguishing among homophones such as 'their' and 'there'. They also misspell the words where some alphabet is silent like'psychology'. Dyslexic children do not recognize the fact that some words are spelt differently from how they are spoken.
- *Limited Vocabulary:* Dyslexic children have good verbal vocabulary but their written vocabulary is very limited.
- *Hand Writing:* Since the children with dyslexia find it difficult to distinguish letters/ numbers/words properly, they have problems with their handwriting also. They write very slowly, their letters may not be very clear or consistent.

OTHER DIFFICULTIES

Spatial Ability

Children with a learning problem may have difficulty in understanding the directions and locating new places. They may also lack spatial ability which may hamper their chances of being good architects. Left, right, front and back and areas of directionality are a weakness among the learning disabled. Many will get lost easily in large buildings, new locations and their poor sense of directionality will cause some confusion. They do not seem to have an intuitive sense for right or left or directions like North, South, East and West. In school, they may not perform well in physical education classes where a number of instructions are given indicating 'directions'. If they are asked to turn left or right they may get confused. Learning disabled children do not know how to read a map since they do not understand the directions. It is very difficult for them to move around the town with a map showing directions. They may forget from which direction they came and in which they are to go. Similarly, these persons may find it difficult to drive as they may forget which way they have to move or from whch direction the traffic would come.

Learning-disabled children find it difficult to perform mechanical jobs. They do not have proper concepts of spatial relationships. Therefore, they may not be good architects. In case they are asked to solve puzzle they may do it through trial and error instead of doing it with a planned sequential approach. They may lose their articles somewhere in the house or elsewhere and may not remember where they have kept them. They may also find it difficult to arrange their belongings in an orderly manner. Things in their room may be scattered all over the place.

Continuous help may improve spatial awareness and sense of directionality over time. Here it is important to mention that all learning disabled children may not suffer from this problem.

Motor Skills

It has been observed that some of the learning disabled lack motor skills. They have poor hand-motor coordination. Holding a pencil or pen in hand is difficult for them, they hold it inappropriately. This is one of the reasons that their handwriting is not legible. They may also find it difficult to perform the mechanical operations as they may not be able to hold the equipments properly. It may be difficult for them to do science practicals holding the apparatus appropriately. Such children either should be given apparatuses suiting to their problems or they should do the work under proper supervision. They should not be left on their own as they could hurt themselves. The movement of their hands may not be according to the movement of their legs. Wherever there is a need to use both the hands together in a sequenced manner, the learning disabled may find it difficult.

Dealing With Mathematics

Learning disabled children may be good in oral maths but due to poor reading skills they may not be so good in written maths. They might face problems in dealing with descriptive mathematics, engineering, or physics problems that rely on written text rather than numbers or formulas. Individuals with learning problems may also have difficulty remembering mathematical facts, such as multiplication tables, learning the sequence of steps when performing calculations, such as long division, and other mathematics which involve remembering the order in which numbers appear. This may be exhibited by having a slow response in mathematical drills and difficulty with word problems.

Dealing With Creativity

The learning disabled may be creative. They can be good leaders, decision makers, artists, painters or thinkers. They can run good businesses. It is necessary to identify their talents and provide opportunities for nurturing their talents. There is no child who does not possess one or the other ability. Instead of rebuking and scolding the child for not performing like others, his ability should be identified, recognised and he should given an opportunity to develop.

Problems in Memory

Memory involves visual memory as well as auditory memory. Learning disabled children are weak in both types of memories. They watch a thing but forget very soon what they saw. Similarly, they hear but they forget what they have heard. They cannot repeat what they saw or heard. Because of this memory disorder their learning process is very slow.

How to Teach Learning-disabled Children

PRE-REQUISITES TO EDUCATE A LEARNING-DISABLED CHILD

Learning disabled children need special attention according to their specific problem. The normal universal curriculum may not suit them. Before drawing up a curriculum and finalizing the strategies of teaching for the learning disabled child, it is necessary to find out the specific problem of the child. As stated earlier, all children with learning difficulties are not the same. It is, therefore, necessary to devise teaching strategies appropriate to the problem of the child. Some pre-requisites for planning teaching for the children with learning difficulties have been discussed in the following pages.

1. Identification of Problem

The first essential step in educating a child with learning difficulty is to identify his specific problem. When the child scores high on intelligence tests but does not perform accordingly, he is scolded by the teacher who think that the child is not giving due attention to studies. Parents also have the same view and insist upon the child to study more and more. In such cases, proper diagnosis of the problem is extremely important. The problem may be one of learning language or writing or in solving mathematical questions. His writing may be illegible. He may not be able to sequence the concepts. He may have speech problem or in remembering dates or figures. Remedial measures can be taken only when the problem area and specific problem of the child are identified.

2. Special Educator

To deal with such a child, there is a need to have a special educator who is aware of the learning problems and techniques to deal with them. Children with learning problems require individual attention and, therefore, individual educational plan is needed. They can be integrated with the normal children but special educators should be there along with the normal school teacher in the class. The school teachers may be given specific training to deal with such children in the class. Team teaching can also be planned in such cases. In case this is not economical or the school's resources do not permit, remedial teaching after the normal class can be planned or provision can be made for an itinerant teacher.

3. Interaction with Parents

Parents should be made aware of the problem of the child so that they can be supportive and cooperative and supplement the efforts in the school. They should also be trained in how to deal with the child. Unlike in case of other disabilities like blindness or deafness, learning disabilities are not apparently visible. They are a disguised problem. It is difficult to convince the parents why even after having good intelligence rating, the child is unable to perform. More and more literature should be developed in various languages to provide information to the parents about the learning disabilities.

4. Learning Material and Readiness of the School

Schools should have adequate teaching material with which the learning-disabled children can 'do themselves' instead of listening to instructions. Multi-sensory approach has to be used to educate the learning-disabled child. Schools should be equipped well to use such techniques. Teaching should be in such a manner that the child could relate it with his daily life experiences. It is extremely essential that schools are ready to accept children who have learning problems. Due to competition and the desire to excel in results, often schools ask such children to take admission in some other school in spite of the Inclusive Education Policy. Schools should have access to resources that would be required to deal with such children, such as trained teachers, adequate budget, services of psychologist and other team members etc.

TEACHING THE LEARNING-DISABLED CHILD

To think that a child with learning difficulty cannot do anything is not correct. With proper assistance and help, most children with learning problems are able to overcome their problems. If the school is aware of the problem and adopts appropriate strategies, the child can stay in the regular classroom and learn with the help of a specially trained teacher, or reading specialist. A team consisting of psychologist, pediatrician, an education therapist or an academic language therapist — who is trained to work with children with learning difficulties, is extremely helpful in dealing with their problems. Specific learning difficulties and the strategies for the teaching of learning disabled have been discussed in the chapters:

(i) Reading

Reading involves coordination of Eyes, Ears and Brain in the Following Manner:

1. Child has to focus on printed material of alphabets and words.
2. He is supposed to concentrate on the whole written page, which requires control of eye movements.
3. He has to practice to recognize the way letters sound
4. Child should understand words and grammar and how the words are put together to construct a sentence.
5. He has to build images and put the associated ideas with the images together.
6. He has to accumulate new material and new ideas to what is already known to him.
7. He has to store all the old and new ideas in his memory.

To teach reading innovative techniques can be evolved. The children might learn new ways of remembering sounds. For example, "p" and "b" are called brother sounds because they are both "lip poppers." One has to press lips together to make the sound. Thinking about the way the mouth needs to move to make sounds can help learning problem kids read more easily.

(ii) Development of Abstract Reasoning

Many learning disabled children lack the ability of abstract reasoning. Sometimes they have their own logic, which may not match with that of the rest of the children. This reasoning ability can be developed through providing opportunities to these children to explore the world themselves and state their experiences in their own words. They may be asked to read a small story along with pictures and then answer simple questions based on their understanding of the story. They may first be asked to answer the questions after seeing the pictures, and in the next step the pictures may be removed and the children allowed to answer on their own. They may be provided with two pictures of similar kind with some variations and be asked to find out similarities and differences in the two pictures. To make it simpler, models of similar kind may be given with some variation. Another method can be to keep the things of similar nature in a box with one or two variations and asked them to sort out those things according to the similarity. For example, fruits and vegetables may be put together in a box and students asked to identify and keep the fruits on one side and vegetables on the other side.

Some children with learning problems enjoy drawing pictures on the paper or make stories on their own, even though such pictures and stories may not have much meaning in them. Such children should be encouraged. They should be asked about the theme of the lines they have drawn or should be encouraged to make stories. Some simple questions in between may be asked to give direction to their thought process.

(iii) Teaching Spellings

Children with learning difficulties can learn to work out the spellings of words that follow a logical pattern of letter sounds (like 'b-a-t' and 's-a-t). The best help for such children is to use phonetics-based teaching of spelling. However, the spellings of words with little relation to their sounds - like 'should' and 'ought' are particularly difficult to remember. They do not sound like the letter-sounds from which they are spelt. In other words the spellings that are written exactly the way these are spoken are easier for the learning disabled child to learn but the spellings that have silent alphabets or written differently than these are spoken are difficult for them. The work 'knife' does not indicate that it starts from 'k'. The child may not remember the spellings of such words. John Bradford (2003) discussed about teaching of dyslexics by using mnemonics. "...tricky words can be learned as a 'mnemonic' by dyslexic children. 'Because', for example, can be remembered from the first letters of the 'silly' sentence: '**B**ig **E**lephants **C**an **A**dd **U**p **S**ums **E**asily'. The word 'any' can be remembered by using the 'silly sentence '**A**nts **N**ever **Y**awn'."

Correcting spellings by consulting a dictionary would not help as these children would not know which alphabet they have to search for. The teacher should write for the dyslexic the spellings of the difficult words on the board, or show them through a Power Point presentation or a chart.

(iv) Writing Sentences

Writing sentences involves not only use of proper words but also good punctuation like use of capital words, use of commas, full stops and other marks that make a sentence complete and convey the proper message. A wrong use of comma can destroy the meaning to be communicated. Learning-disabled children are weak in using such punctuations or writing complete sentences. They often omit punctuation marks. To teach sentence writing, the teacher should choose a paragraph with small sentences which are relatively easy and the child can understand and read. The sentences may be written without punctuation and the child asked if he could understand the meaning of the written material. Afterwards, the teacher may start punctuating the sentences one by one. The child may be asked to practice till he perfects the punctuation. The same paragraphs should be repeated for a few days to practice punctuation. Gradually, the child learns the punctuation and can start writing sentences on his own correctly.

Another method of teaching sentence writing to a dyslexic is to say two sentences and tell the child that these are two sentences. For example:

1. Today I went to market.
2. I purchased mango

When the child counts that these are two sentences, teacher can teach how these could be made one putting 'and' in between. Child understands how with the use of 'and' two sentences can be joined. By joining such small sentences the child learns to make sentences. It is necessary that the teacher identifies the small and easy sentences and teaches how to join them. The child should be given practice on one type of conjunction first before teaching him another.

(v) Speech Problem

The children suffering with speech problems or reading skills should be taught with patience and using multi-sensory techniques. To explain the words, audio-visual material can be used as, for example, to teach the child the names of the vegetables, the models of different vegetables may be brought to the classroom. Story-telling is another method through which children identify themselves and can learn language. Saying a small sentence or word may be demonstrated and child should be asked to repeat the word or sentence. Researches conducted in Stanford University, USA show that music helps in developing skills in language. Researches have also found that the people who listen to music can differentiate minor differences in word syllables. It has also been found that musical training helps in efficient working up of the brain to process the language as there are rapidly changing sounds. Gabrieli said that the brain is adaptable and trainable.

(vi) Improving Handwriting

Children suffering with learning difficulty have uneven handwriting which many a time is difficult to understand. They confuse between similar kind of letters. While writing, they forget which way to place the curve for writing an alphabet. For example, it is difficult for them to remember how to make the bend for d or b or p or q and so on. If this problem is severe it is described as 'dysgraphia'. The children who find it difficult to hold the pen properly write in a very zig-zag manner. They can also suffer with poor motor control, tension, problem of writing slow etc.

The children who have writing disability or a poor handwriting should be helped in a number of ways. They should be taught the hand and finger exercises so that their muscles could be strengthened. Multiple materials should be provided to them to practice the writing. Initially they may be given some small beads and asked to write alphabets or words using the beads. They can be given clay and asked to prepare alphabets using the clay. Later, they may be asked to write using a chalk on blackboard. Some lines may be drawn on the board and the child taught to write using these lines as boundaries. The child should be taught how to hold a pen or pencil, how to keep the note book before him, the direction in which it should be placed, etc. and should be helped in writing to practice the alphabets. Another method is to keep various alphabets in a box and ask the child to find out a specific alphabet, keep that alphabet on the note book and draw lines with the pen. As a second step, he may keep this alphabet before him and try to write on the copy on his own. The child should not be asked to proceed further till he masters writing the alphabet in the proper manner because once he is moved further he may not be able to improve his handwriting or master the alphabets already learnt. He should be taught how much distance he should leave between two alphabets or words. Note book with space lines may be used for developing good handwriting. Alphabets in various colours, material of different shapes should be used with dyslexic children to motivate them and attract them towards these materials.

Handwriting of dyslexic children can be improved if they are taught to write in cursive hand writing.

If the child is unable to pickup, help of modern educational technologies like computers can be taken. Such children should be allowed to write through laptops or computers with the software for checking spellings. This would boost the confidence of the children and they will not feel isolated in the class. Audiotapes can be used for recording lessons, which can then be written down at a later stage. Written record of the pupil's verbal account or voice—activated software can be used.

Children can be asked to observe their writing, tell what they have written and examine how they can write better. Self-analysis and criticism will save them from the humiliation of external criticism. Class talks by a school counselor or other experts can be arranged on how to develop good handwriting or importance of good handwriting. Children can be demonstrated how a child with better handwriting gets better scores than the child whose handwriting is illegible. It should be ensured that a chart of alphabets/ and common words is available with each child as an aid of memory for the cursive script in upper and lower case. Practice should be given on the words the child can write well and understand its meaning.

(vii) Writing Paragraphs

When a learning disabled child is asked to write a paragraph or essay or a story or a write-up on any topic like a visit to zoo or garden, he may find it problematic, as he cannot sequence the events. A better way would be to give him an outline and ask to develop these points into paragraphs. Another approach is to ask them to prepare an outline. Teacher can check the sequencing of the outline and then ask to write details of each sub-topic.

For example an essay on 'Dog as a Friend' can have following outline on which children can develop the details:

1. Introduction – Writing about animal.
2. Various types of animals.
3. Types of pet animals.
4. How dog as a pet animal is helpful.
5. How to maintain a dog—his food, hygiene etc.
6. How I play with my pet dog.
7. How I teach my dog to learn.
8. Why dog is my friend.
9. Precautions.

Such a plan can develop writing skills in a child with learning problems.

(viii) Teaching Mathematics

Special techniques are to be used to educate learning disabled children depending upon their specific problems. In case a student is having problems in mathematical abilities, the problems should not be ignored. The curriculum should be suitably adapted as well as multiple methods of teaching should be used. The learning disabled students may have trouble in remembering the basic number facts. Instead of using memory to do the four elementary arithmetic operations of addition, subtraction, multiplication and division, such as 3+2 = 5 or 6-3 = 3 or 2 x 3 = 6, they try to count on fingers or through some objects like beads. They find it difficult to do the four basic arithmetic operations. In such cases, instead of insisting that the child should do these operations mentally they should be allowed to keep beads or some other objects for this purpose or to use simple charts for doing these operations so that they could move further alongwith the class. Intensive practice is required for disabled students to attain mastery on the concepts. Practice sessions should be of short duration instead of long streaches. For example, a practice streatch of 10 to 15 minutes' duration would be more effective than asking the child to practice half an hour or one hour. Sums should be given on simple and reverse operations for example 2+3 = 5 and 3+2 = 5. One operation at a time like 2+3 = 5, 2+4 = 6 should be taught. Some other disabled children easily understand the mathematical concepts but are weak in calculations. The curriculum involves the sequence of steps, which they may forget. This weakness of the students should be recognized. Sometimes, emphasis is given only on calculations. This would not be correct. In case the child is weak in calculations but otherwise has ability, his efforts should be given encouragement. A self-monitoring system can be developed or double check system should be taught to the child so that he could find out mistakes he is making in the calculations. Some other learning disabled children may have difficulty with visual– motor coordination or difficulty with the material that is depicted through pictures. They confuse in numbers in signs and other symbols. Such students require very specific and clear verbal instructions. Instead of presenting the concepts through pictures or diagrams or charts it is better to explain them verbally. The verbal instrument may follow the replicas of objects. For example, they may be given a square and told to count the sides to teach that a square has four sides. Sometimes, it is difficult for such children to apply their routine arithmetic knowledge to the methods which are used in the syllabus of the school. In such cases the examples used in the syllabus should be selected from those a student comes across during his daily life. The models, the structures, etc with which the student is familiar may be used.

Mathematics requires a number of operations to be performed mentally, which children with learning difficulty find it difficult. It uses symbols and a new language, which the child with learning-disability finds difficult to learn. It is not necessary that all the children have problems in learning mathematics or all its branches. Some are excellent in attempting mathematical problems. A dyslexic child may be good in one branch of mathematics while he may be weak in another branch. It has been estimated that around 90 per cent of dyslexic children have problems in at least some areas of mathematicss. Many children have problems in areas like multiplication tables, fractions, decimals, percentages, ratios and statistics. Sometimes, the very simple process of counting or reverse counting is difficult for them. Such students usually need extra instructions, particularly as new concepts are introduced.

First of all, mathematical terminology and language used in the area in which the child is facing the problem has to be taught to the child. The calculation part has to be taken later, once the child becomes fully acquainted with the terminology of the subject. In other words, processes involved like addition, subtraction etc. should be taught at a later stage. The learning disabled child can also face difficulties with the sums that require a number of steps or are lengthy. Moreover, the child should be taught how to use his own logic to check his answers for the question he has solved.

Here are some guidelines, which can help, in teaching mathematics to a child with learning disabilities.

- Teach concepts sequentially and in small steps. The syllabus should be divided into very small parts. One small step at a time should be taught and the child should be asked to practice till he gets mastery over it. For example, to teach counting the child should be taught the counting of two numbers of one digit level-1+1 =? 1+2=? And so on. Once the child can do it, he may be taught one digit and two digit level numbers-1+10=? Later on he may be introduced with counting of three numbers such as 1+1+4=?

- Do not move to the second part or concept until the student is ready and thoroughly understands the concept taught earlier. For example, do not move on to counting backwards until basic counting has been mastered.
- Introduce games to teach mathematics, so that it could be a fun activity. For example, the child can be given chocolates and can be asked to count or the chocolates can be placed on the floor and the child can be asked to distribute five chocolates to each child. Use of beads in counting can also be fun. Children can put ten beads in a string.
- For teaching multiplication and division, Jean Herold mentions a technique— 'collect 5 pairs of items, gloves, shoes, toy animals, anything as long as the pairs are the same. Lay out the pairs in front of the child, show her that there are two items in each pair, one pair has two items, two pairs have four items, etc. When the child sees the five pairs have ten items, explain as you write it down, that is what 5 x 2=10 means. This exercise can be repeated with each of the different pairs until she understands what "2 times" means. Once the child is familiar with the 2 times table, they should begin to work on all the tables in the following order: 2x, 10x, 11x, 5x, 3x, 4x, 9x, 6x, 7x, 8x, then finally 12x, which they should know from the other tables.' It should be kept in mind that while using this technique items with which the child is familiar should be used.
- Mathematical concepts can be taught narrating some story and keeping some objects to show along with the story. This is a multi sensory approach, which is very effective in teaching the dyslexics.
- Mathematics through games can do wonders with dyslexic child. Games can be of various types using several types of material/people. Innovative games can be thought of to teach several concepts of mathematics. Simple games can be to ask the child make a team of three children/ five

children or ten children each to play a particular game. Another game could be to ask the children to pick up balls from the floor and put it in the baskets. After the allotted time finishes, each team asked to count the balls. These techniques can be used to teach counting. With variation in this game the teacher can tech other processes also. Bingo is very popular among dyslexic children. Make a Bingo type card on a piece of paper; fill the squares with the answers to all the multiplication facts, up to 6 x 6 with regular dice, 9 x 9 and 12 x 12. Take it in turns to roll the dice; multiply the two numbers rolled and mark it off on the players' Bingo sheets. A number of computer games are available which can be used for teaching purposes.

- To develop auditory and visual memory, children should be asked to speak what they are doing in solving the maths question. This is known as talk through technique
- Mathematics can be taught using a calculator. After doing the questions using normal techniques, students can check the answers using a calculator. It is important that whenever the dyslexic child does some question correctly, he should be encouraged, mistakes should be pointed out in a manner so that child does not feel humiliated or frustrated.
- Dyslexic child can be taken to the market and can be taught to buy things of need with the money. He can learn addition and subtraction then and there in practical terms. Wherever possible real life situations should be created to teach the child. Visual objects should be used to teach different concepts. For example, to teach the concepts of 'circle', 'square' etc. coloured cutouts could be shown to the students.
- Put key words on a card index system or on the inside cover of the pupil's note book so that it can be used for reference and revision.
- Rehearse mathematical vocabulary constantly, using multi sensory/kinesthetic methods.
- Put the decimal point in red ink. It helps visual perception with the dyslexic child.

These are some of the methods that can be adopted to teach learning disabled. Many more innovative methods can be evolved with experience and experiments.

Role of Parents, Schools and Community

In assisting children with learning disabilities to overcome their difficulties and improve their learning process, the parents, the school and the community at large have a key role to play. As stated earlier the first important step for the parents and the teachers in the school is to recognize children with learning disabilities and to identify their specific problem. Apart from learning difficulties, dyslexics may face difficulty in having inter-personal relations or social interactions. Their problems can range from mild to extreme in their severity.

Summary Table of Problems of Dyslexic Children

Category	*Conditions*	*Examples*
1. Visual Problems	Poor visual memory	Not remembering faces, words, people's names, reversals in writing (41 instead of 14)
	Poor visual perception	Difficulty in seeing the difference between similar objects (b and d)
	Figure ground discrimination	Inability to find the place to write one's name on an application form
	Poor visual tracking	Inability to follow a line on a page
2. Auditory Problems	Poor auditory memory	Difficulty in remembering what has been said, information or instructions
	Poor auditory discrimination	Difficulties in telling the difference between similar sounds, e.g. bee and pea or seventy and seventeen
	Poor auditory sequencing	Confusion with number sequence, lists or directions
	Poor auditory figure ground	Trouble hearing sounds over background noises

(Contd.)

Category	Conditions	Examples
3. Motor Problems	Poor eye-hand coordination	Difficulties with handwriting
	Poor small muscle control	Misjudging where to place things
	Poor large muscle control	Clumsiness
4. Organi-sational Problems	Poor time management	Inability to be punctual, to meet deadlines
	Poor ability to organize tasks	Not understanding the steps required to carry out a task
	Poor ability to organize space	Inability to arrange things in a cupboard, a desk, arranging matter in a page
	Impairment of executive function	Inability to analyse things or apply information in a new situation
5. Conceptual Problems	Difficulty in interpret-ting non-verbal language	Facial expressions or body language
	Difficulty in understan-ding figures of speech	Idioms, metaphors, similes
	Difficulties in anticipating future	Doing things without assessing consequences
	Rigid thinking	Inability to be flexible in thinking
	Poor social skills and peer relations	Not maintaining eye contact during conversation, using inappropriate tone or language, lacking social graces

It may be mentioned that a person with learning disability in one area may be very successful in other areas.

WHAT THE FAMILY SHOULD DO

Parents feel embarrassed when they see that their child is not performing as well as other children of his age or class. This attitude is not correct. It is important for them to understand and accept that every child, whether a slow-learner or not, needs love, affection, praise and motivation. Parents should find out the likes and dislikes of their child and should encourage and appreciate for every effort made by him, whether big or small. A dyslexic child needs constant support and praise to gain self-esteem. One of the biggest problems for the dylexic child is that he may never have the opportunity to discover his strengths because he is always pointed out and nagged for his mistakes.

Family is the first base for every child. Therefore, development of the child depends upon how he is handled by the family members including parents, siblings and other members of the extended family. Family provides a kind of support system to the children. In the modern days, when joint family system is breaking up and nuclear families are emerging to an increasing degree, role of parents and brothers and sisters is very important in the overall development of the children. Children with disabilities have special needs and they require to be handled with greater care and concern. If, since the beginning, the disability of the child is accepted in the family and he is given proper support, he can develop as a normal person. The following are some of the precautions that should be taken in dealing with disabled children at the family level.

(i) Understanding the Disability

If, in a family, there is a learning-disabiled child, parents should try to get more and more information about the disability. Precautionary measures should be taken so that the disability would not increase and adequate measures should be taken to deal with the disability. The information so collected should be shared with other family members. The parents should also contact the concerned doctors, psychologist and wherever possible should take training in dealing with their child. Newer researches are coming up. Newer methodologies and resources are being invented to teach the learning disabled and make them independent. Parents should have knowledge of these researches, methodologies and resources and access them to help their child.

(ii) Acceptance of the Child With his Disability

If the family members accept the child with his disability, it provides a lot of support to the child and he can face the challenges with greater self-confidence, acceptance and awareness. Parents and other family members should not pass negative comments about the disability of the child, rather they should encourage him to cope with his disability and help him in making necessary adjustments to overcome his problems. Parents have to provide all kinds to emotional and moral support besides educational support.

(iii) Identification of Specific Skills

Family should try to identify the special capabilities of their learning disabiled child. Each and every person is endowed with some kind of specific skill, which should be identified and nurtured. For example, the child may be a good painter; may be able to make good models, or has a good ear for music. Arrangements should be made for providing training in the identified field where he has potential to excel. The school authorities should also be informed about the special ability of the child so that school also may provide special training to the child.

(iv) Guidance and Supervision

Parents or family members should know how much their child requires guidance and supervision. In case of need, some special institutional help may be sought so that family could deal with their child adequately. Parents should neither be over-protective nor under-protective because of the disability of the child. The family should try to make the child self-dependent. More supervision and guidance may be necessary in the early childhood and, as the child grows up, the extent of supervision could be reduced. Proper leaning atmosphere should be created in the family. While parents have to play a pro-active role, the help of a trained person should be taken where necessary to deal with learning problems of the child,

(v) Providing Proper Facilities

When the problem of the child is identified, family should support the child in its assessment and measuring the capacities the child has. Appropriate aids and appliances should be provided so that the child could manage his life by himself to the extent possible. Family should also facilitate the integration of the child in the society as well as in the school by interacting with the concerned people. Since the child interacts with the family first, the impression given by the family would be lasting on him.

(vi) Family and the Emotional Needs of the Disabled

The family has to deal with the child's feelings of guilt and dejection. Parents and other members should explain to the child that there are individual differences and variations and it is not his fault if he is not able to learn fast. They should explain to him what special abilities he has. The child should be encouraged to pursue normal education. The parents have to divide their time between the child in difficulty and the other children in the house according to their respective needs. If the parents are adaptive to the situation, the learning disabiled child could be made to feel normal and that would enable his development as a normal personality. It should be remembered that these children require normal love and affection and not pity or sympathy.

(vii) Day to day Activities

A learning disabiled child may need help in performing his daily activities and learning skills. Family has to tell him very specifically what to do. This has to be told in specific small steps. For example if they want the child that he should put all the things of his room in order they should be specific. e.g. Pick up the dirty clothes and put them for laundry; pick up book and place them on the table/ bag; collect all the games or toys scattered in the room and put them at their proper place etc.

(viii) Management Skills

Parents can teach the child to develop self management skills while the child performs his day-to-day work. Some examples of how to teach such skills can be as follows:

- Teaching the child to use a map, learn the bus routes, hiring a public transport, buying things from the market.
- Teaching the child to cook
- Teaching the child to use a spoon, napkin, placing of plate and glass etc.
- Teaching him how to count the money, keep an account, how to budget.
- Teaching the child the home phone number, emergency numbers and how to dial numbers; answer the phone politely and to take messages.

A learning disabled child needs more time to complete tasks, as well as some additional time between difficult tasks; thus parents have to deal very patiently with such children. Because of their short attention span, learning disabiled children are not able to complete their homework as per schedule. They should be allowed to take several breaks while working on a task. Too much noise or movement around easily distracts dyslexic children. Parents can help by removing all distractions and by keeping the room fairly quiet when the child is at work.

Children with learning disabilities are generally also averse to examinations, as they are not able to complete the paper in the allotted time. Parents can be of great help in developing a test-taking habit in the child. Parents can give simple tests of short duration so that the child can do it without being restless. Thus, he can learn to organize himself during examinations. Pointing out answers which are wrong, asking the child to read the subject again, and having the child explain the answer helps him relax.

ROLE OF THE SCHOOL

School is the second home for the children. Whatever the child learns at home is strengthened and complemented in the school, which results in total personality development of the child. School environment has to be friendly and harmonious for the child in difficulty. Dyslexic children require mainstreaming and integration with the other school children. These children may require special attention according to their specific problem but they should not be isolated from other children of the school. Children with severe problems require intensive continuous intervention. In the regular classroom, special tutorials with direct and repeated instructions would be helpful. Training in social skills, use of equipment to overcome learning problems, practice in speaking and writing, and adapted curriculum should be provided. Behaviour management is another area which should be given due attention. Patience is required in dealing with such students. They should be encouraged to adopt appropriate behaviours. Simple assignments should be given and students should not be punished for their slow pace of learning. The special assistance should be reduced in a phased manner when the child is able to overcome his learning problem. The school can play a positive role in the development of the learning disabled children in the following manner.

1. Creating Awareness

Children with learning disabilities have to live with other normal children but the other children may not understand the special needs of these children. It is the responsibility of the school that a proper atmosphere is created for the integration of the children with disabilities with their peer group of normal children. This is possible through awareness generation programmes. On the one hand, it would provide information to each and all about various types of problems the child has and, on the other, this awareness would be helpful in responding to the special needs of the child. The peer group also would learn to welcome the children with learning problems. This awareness generation may be done through screening of films, organizing plays, providing written material, etc. The teachers may also ask the students some questions to assess their knowledge about disabilities and how they would deal with them. There are a lot of misconceptions about dyslexic children, which can be overcome in the school situation through awareness generation programmes.

2. Group Participation

Keeping the dyslexic child isolated, when other children are participating in-group activities, is not a healthy practice. The school should encourage the child to participate in various activities, be it group discussions, other group work or extra curricular activities. There are instances when these children, if encouraged, can do wonders one cannot think of.

3. Adaption of the School Curriculum

Some modifications are required in the school curriculum and also in the teaching styles. If there are children with learning diabilities in the class, writing on the blackboard should be followed by the verbal communication. The children with problems of sight may be allowed to learn in Braille or to use a tape-recorder. Computers may be provided to such students.

4. Teacher's Training

Special training for teachers in recognizing specific learning disabilities and dealing with children with such disabilities to integrate them with normal children is extremely necessary, which the school should arrange. The children do not require sympathy but need empathy. Pity does not help in the development of the children with disabilities. Encouraging participation without discrimination, normal communication with them, their acceptance and care on the part of the teachers are important factors.

5. Medical Facilities

Most schools have some first-aid facilities. Some schools have arrangement for a medical center and a provision for a regular doctor. Wherever a regular doctor is not available, visits by a doctor on certain specified days is arranged. Periodic medical tests are also organized. Some schools also keep contact with a nearby hospital. The children with learning disabilities who require medical facilities should be identified and referred to the doctor/hospital or other referral facilities. The school can maintain a record of such services available and whenever required these sources can be contacted and children can be helped.

6. Counselling

A child may face difficulties during its interaction with the peer group in the school. Provision should be made for a Counsellor to deal with emotions and hang-ups of the children with disabilities. While in some of the schools advisory services of a Counsellor are available, others with no such regular facilities can take the help of Counselors posted in other schools. Counsellors can also help in discussing the problem of the child with the parents.

7. Identification and Assessment of the Child

In the ideal situation, the family would know about the disability of the child and would be providing all sorts of needed help. But in a number of cases, the family is unaware of the problem of the child or, even when aware, due to ignorance they do not pay much attention to it. As has been stated earlier, it is not easy to detect a learning disability. Parents are totally ignorant and scold children for not learning. In some other cases where there are broken families, children are neglected. In such circumstances it is the responsibility of the school to observe the children, identify and assess the extent of their problem. School should also keep in touch with the family to get the facts about the child's history or apprise the family members. The schools can also organize small workshops for parents on the children's problems and how to deal with them.

8. Holistic Approach

The schools have to adopt a holistic approach and provide services to the children with special needs. Schools should have services for continual assessment of the problem and needs of the child, medical facilities, guidance and counseling facilities, interaction with parents, provision for adaptation of school facilities, training of teachers, resource center, remedial teaching and so on. There may be a need for speech therapist, or a medical doctor. Such facilities should be available with the school. The school may also have to have liaison with community resources including vocational training centers, employers, rehabilitation centers, sheltered workshops and NGOs so that children with special needs could be helped after they go out of the school system.

ROLE OF COMMUNITY

All children have to develop as responsible adults. Each and every child is a part of community whatever his or her disability may be. It is the responsibility of the community to provide a congenial atmosphere so that every child could get an equal opportunity to develop. Some of the steps a community can take in this direction are detailed below:

(i) Mapping of Resources

A resource mapping should be done at community level, which can be utilized for helping the disabled. These resources may be the special education teachers, special doctors, the physiotherapists, the hospitals, the education institutions, vocational training institutes and places where aids and appliances for disabled are available, financial institutions that may help the disabled, other institutional support such as sheltered workshops for mentally retarded or institutional homes for severely mentally challenged people, etc. The community should also know about the counselling centers available at the nearby places. This information may be collected by Residents Welfare Associations of the community, panchayat offficials, NGOs or even ordinary residents of the community. Community should also have the information about types of learning disabled children in the community and their needs.

(ii) Dissemination of the Information

The information so collected by the community should be available for all the people. This can be disseminated through the notice board, through the pamphlets, inviting the residents for a meeting, etc. The community should help the families where there is a dyslexic child. Change in mindsets of the people is a pre-requisite for rehabilitation of the children with specific needs, which can be done adopting indirect methods like organising street plays in the community, organizing competition where the dyslectic child can show his capability. This would also help mainstreaming of the dyslexic child.

(iii) Awareness Generation

Awareness generation programmes should also be organized at community level so that not only parents understand the disabilities of their child but also some level of acceptance is generated in the community for acceptance of such disabilities.

(iv) Integration of Disabled in the Community

A variety of efforts are to be made by various communities to integrate the disabled child in the mainstream. There are instances where communities celebrate various festivals together or competitions are organized at community level where all children participate. Such activities help in removing the misconceptions about various disabilities.

(v) Volunteer Services

Community can help in providing volunteer services to the disabled children. For example, a dyslexic student may need the services of a volunteer who can help in doing practice in writing. A volunteer from the community may help him for this purpose. Volunteers may also work for motivating the child in participating in community activity. Community workers may also help integration of the child in the school.

(vi) Attitudinal Change

As has been discussed elsewhere, positive attitudes are important for normal growth of the child. Favourable attitudes facilitate positive personality development. The attitude change may come from the awareness about the disability and removal of stereotype prejudices against disabled. For this purpose, film shows may be organized at community level. Talks by experts, by doctors, etc. may also help in attitudinal changes. Sometimes, community people have a lot of queries about disabilities. In such a situation it is necessary that community meetings are organized where a doctor or a specialist may be invited to interact with the people. Some success stories where disabled people could do things as normal children do may also help in bringing about an attitudinal change of the people.

Summary Table

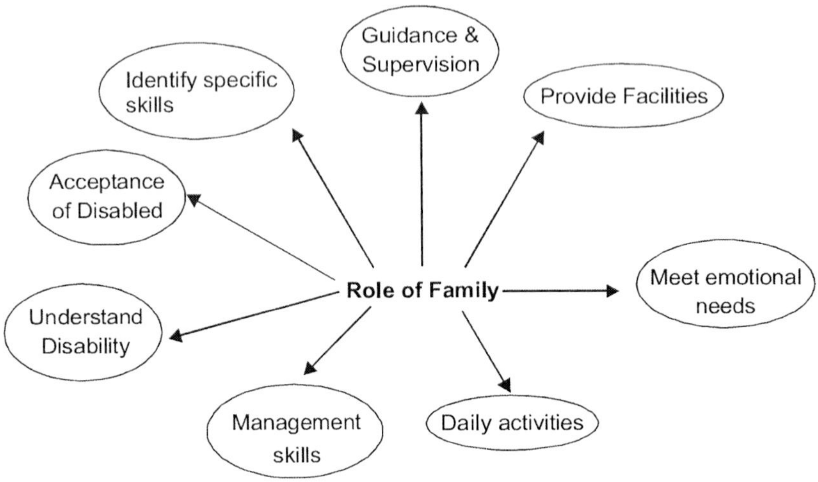

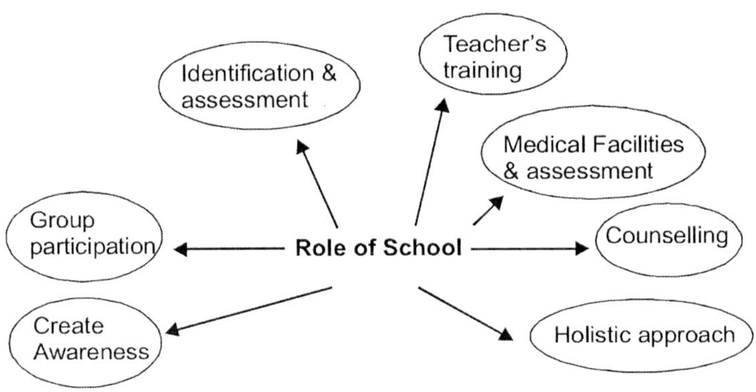

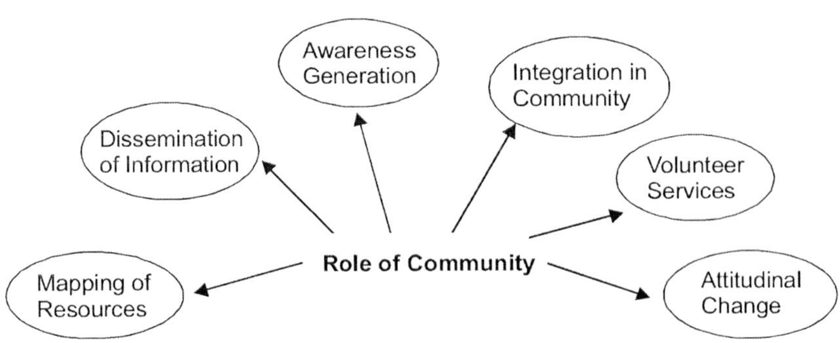

How Teachers should Deal with Learning Disabled Children

For bringing about modification in behaviour of the learning disabled child, he should be observed in various situations to understand about his strengths and problems. These situations can be his interactions with other students, group activities, games, the classroom, group discussions, etc. When the child shows positive social behaviour, it should be recognized and reinforced. This reinforcement can be through verbal or non-verbal communication. Verbal communication may include encouraging words like 'you are doing well' or 'it was excellent', etc. Non-verbal communication can be a pat on the back of the child, a smile or similar positive body gestures. On the other hand, when he is not behaving in a socially desirable manner, some signaling system which the child understands should be established to communicate this fact. This does not mean that the teacher should punish the child. One can communicate the undesirableness of the child's behaviour through signals like touching the child with hand or touching of your own finger or any other symbolic gesture, which the child gradually follows and modifies his behaviour. This technique is helpful in developing self-confidence in the child, as he does not get punished before others.

In many cases, children with learning diabilities forget to bring the required material like pencil, scale or an eraser to the school. Instead of scolding the child, it is better to keep an extra set of the material in the school and make it available to the child, and collecting it back when the class is over. Social skills can be taught through T.V. shows, dramas, role-play, etc. To get the attention of all the children, innovativeness on the part of the teacher would be very useful. The teacher may introduce some games to start the lesson or tell some small story, or mayshow some coloured pictures or models. Children will easily be attracted to such methods and pay greater attention to what the teacher is saying. While teaching and using the chalkboard a laser beam should be used to focus on the point. Overhead projectior may be used to catch the attention of the students. The teacher should involve all the students in the class, and group activities should be given according to the abilities of the students. Such activities may not be common for all the students.

The following guidelines for teachers are helpful in dealing with learning disabled:

(A) DEALING IN THE CLASS

- An outline should be given of each topic which the teacher wants to teach in the class. After the teaching is complete, recapitulation should be done. Children should be told what has been taught in the class. Since dyslexics have short-term memory such repetition would help them to remember the lesson and the instructions.
- When homework is given, the teacher should ensure that the child has noted down the work to be done correctly. Wherever needed the teacher should write down in the child's diary what homework the child is required to do. A note for parents may also be written.
- The child should be encouraged to write down in the diary the telephone numbers of their friends so that in case of need about over homework, they can check with their peers
- The teacher may make a daily checklist for the pupil for reference. The child can refer to the checklist whenever needed. This would make him self-dependent and responsible.
- Activities should be given in small steps.
- If visual memory is poor, copying must be kept to a minimum. In such cases handouts with large letters should be given.
- The child should be made to fairly close to the class teacher so that the teacher is easily available to help if necessary.
- Teacher should use different colour chalks for writing the information on the board,
- Writing on the board should be well spaced.
- Leave the writings on the blackboard for longer time so that the child could copy it easily.
- Teacher should write in cursive style of writing.
- Words written should be very clear.

How to Help in Reading

- A structured reading scheme that involves repetition and introduces new words very gradually is extremely important. The teacher should ensure that the child starts reading simpler words and simpler sentences before moving on to more complex ones.
- Demands from the child should be as per his capacities so that the child may not get depressed and demotivated. The child should not be asked to read a book at a level beyond his current level of skills. If he has to work too hard to read, he will not understand the meaning of what he is reading.
- The teacher should not ask the child to 'read aloud in class'. Reading assignment can be given to him when only the teacher is present. He can also be asked in advance to read the topic at home before it is taught in the class. This will help ensure that the child is seen to be able to read out loud, along with other children
- Spelling rules can be given to the whole class. Words for class spelling tests are often topic-based rather than grouped for structure. If there are one or two dyslexics in the class, a short list of structure-based words for their weekly spelling test will be far more helpful than random words. Three or four irregular words can be included each week. Eventually this would help to improve their free-writing skills.

How to Evaluate the Work Done by Learning Disabled Child

- Evaluation of the child's work should be done taking into account his ideas and creativity. Spelling mistakes or bad handwriting should not be the only criteria for evaluation.
- Spelling mistakes pinpointed should be those appropriate to the child's level of spelling. Marking should be done in pencil with positive comments.
- Comments or marking in red ink should be avoided while assessing the dyslexic child's work.
- Only, the words a dyslexic child has written incorrectly should be given to him to repeat and practice, and not the whole long paragraphs.

How to Assign Homework to a Learning Disabled

Since it takes more time for the learning disabled child to read, learn and understand, he feels tired when the school is over. Home work to such a child should be given so that it does not produce monotony and boredom or remind him of his mistakes. Dyslexics should be given less work compared to other children as they take more time to complete the same.

Acceptance of the Child

Mainstreaming of the child in the class is extremely essential. He should not only be accepted by the teachers but also by fellow students. The teacher can play an important role in the integration of the child in the class. The child should be made comfortable so that he can be a part of the learning environment of the class. For such integration, he should be encouraged to express himself verbally. His ideas should be recognized. It is not advisable that teacher insists on written communication when the child has difficulty in writing. Since the child needs help of some specialist, he should not get a feeling that he is different from others. Help can be provided in the classroom itself. There would be children with varying needs and they may require remedial teaching etc. Different groups can be formed for specific help so that the dyslexic child may not feel isolated.

Class teachers dealing with children with learning disabilities need to be flexible in their approach, so that they can find a method that suits the individual child, rather than expecting that all pupils will learn in the same way. Above all, there must be an understanding among all those who teach them, that they may have many talents and skills. Their abilities must not be measured purely on the basis of their difficulties in acquiring literacy skills. Dyslexic children, like all children, thrive on challenges and success.

WHAT A TEACHER SHOULD NOT DO

The teacher should not force the student to participate in every activity if he is not willing. The dyslexic child should not be compared with other normal children. Failures or slow progress of these children should not be commented upon. Punishment should not be used in general to achieve modifications of the behaviour of the children. In rare circumstances when the child shows behaviours which are harmful to him or others, he can be punished but this punishment should not include corporal punishment. It may be verbal warning initially to modify the behaviour. In no case should corporal punishment be used.

Strategies for Teaching-Learning and Intervention

Education is a Fundamental Right under the Constitution of India. The programme of Sarva Shiksha Abhiyan launched by the government has the goal of educating each and every child without any kind of discrimination. Therefore, children with special needs also have a right to education irrespective of the type of their disability, its degree, category etc. The schools have to provide a congenial environment for all types of children including children with special needs. A 'Zero Rejection' policy has been accepted under Sarva Shiksha Abhiyan. The educational policy of the country stresses the need for integrated education for the disabled children, which indicates that children with disabilities are to be placed in the normal schools along with the other children. Various approaches and methods have been adopted for educating the children with special needs, which include formal and non-formal education, open school system, home based education, remedial teaching, vocational education, arrangement for resource teachers, curriculum adjustment, etc. Teaching—learning strategies and social education provisions with reference to the children with disabilities include a number of components such as curriculum adjustment and adaptation, classroom management, mapping of community resources, teaching strategies etc. These strategies are discussed in detail in the following pages.

(A) CURRICULUM ADJUSTMENT AND ADAPTATION

Let us consider a typical class-room situation. In a class where there are children with learning disabilities, a teacher comes to the class, teaches the topic for the day, gives some home work to be done and leaves the class after the time for the topic is over. Next day, the teacher asks for the homework done by the students, and some students do not submit their workbooks. The teacher scolds them for not doing the work. The basic reason for not doing the work is that these children are not able to understand the lesson taught by the teacher, as these children are suffering from learning disabilities. In this situation, curriculum adjustment and adaptation becomes essential. In case of disabled children the curriculum has to be adapted in a manner close to the real life situation than teaching the topic with a theoretical perspective. The curriculum has to have a practical orientation combined with functions. A theoretical approach to teach a lesson would be to explain the subject matter verbally, while a functional approach would be to show the children practical examples of how the theory works in real life, with situations which they may face or interact with in their lives. For example, in the theoretical method, the teacher may talk about various vegetables and their uses, while in a practical orientation the teacher may bring the specimens of those vegetables, with which the student is familiar at home. Another way may be that the teacher takes the children to the market and asks them to identify the vegetables. In other words, the subject has to be taught to the children in relation to its functional utility.

The general considerations for curriculum modifications would be as follows:

1. Identification of Needs of the Children

The first step for curriculum adjustment is to identify the needs of the children with various disabilities. Their residual capacities are to be assessed and their interacting behaviours are to be mapped. Curriculum has to be modified and adapted according to the levels of abilities and residual capacities,. For example, in case of dyslexics the study material should be presented in large prints in cursive print; curriculum should have focus on oral communication; topics are to be divided in small parts and simple steps, visuals are to be used along with oral communication and so on. The curriculum has to be divided into a small and sequenced set of activities.

2. Holistic Approach to Curriculum

Education in general focuses upon the overall development of children but curriculum has to be very specific in case of disabled children according to their specific needs of development and adjustments required. The curriculum should include topics like self-care, safety measures, use of aids and appliances and their maintenance, mobility training, development of coping strategies for their problems, community and school resources available to them, peer interaction, development of positive self-image and overall personality development. The curriculum has to be so devised that the children who suffer from disability may not have feeling of neglect or self-derogation.

3. Curriculum and Group Interactions

School curriculum is not restricted to teach a topic only. The curriculum should provide ample opportunities for group interaction and participation. There may be situations where at the time of group exercises, the teacher not fully aware about the disability, may ask the disabled child to just observe what is happening in the group and not to participate. Sometimes some teachers make a remark such as 'this child cannot do'. Such attitudes on the part of the teachers develop a sense of negative self in the child. All children should be integrated to participate and interact among each other without any discrimination. The support services, which are necessary for such participation, should be made available to the children in need.

4. Curriculum and Functional Orientation

Curriculum should be related to day-to-day lives of the children. It is more important in case of disabled children. Children would be able to identify better with the things they are familiar with in their day-to-day living. Teaching through such objects/material is easier than quoting the examples of unknown things and material. Things become more difficult for him if the teacher explains the concept of vegetables in abstract manner giving the examples of some vegetables the child has not experienced. More and more visits for outside experience, motivating the other senses should be included in the curriculum for the disabled children. The functional orientation of curriculum involves setting the objectives that would facilitate the functioning of the individual as an independent person. To develop a disabled child as an independent functioning person, specific objectives in terms of skills to be developed should be identified and listed. These skills are to be linked to various tasks in various settings in which the child has to live. These settings are family, school, employment, the community and the society.

5. Adapting Published Material

According to the varying needs of the children with disabilities, the curriculum should be divided into various topics, topics into various concepts and concepts into various skills to be developed in the child. For developing these skills various activities may be planned in the class according to the residual capacities of the children. Here, while adapting the published material, it should be kept in mind that one skill at a time should be developed. If the concept of colour is being taught to learning disabled child, at the first step he should try to learn about one or two colours. Then he should learn about more colours and their differentiations as a next step, their identification at the later stage etc. in a sequential manner. Practice of the same concept is necessary for retention.

Adapting a published material involves the following steps:

1. The total curriculum has to be divided into various topics.
2. Each topic must be divided into various concepts.
3. Each concept should be divided into skills to be developed in the child.
4. Tasks are to be identified according to the skills to be developed. It must be remembered that one skill at a time must be developed.

Special Needs of the Learning Disabled Children

Sl.No..	*Types of needs*	*Curriculum adaptation*
1.	Academic needs	Reading, writing, learning of specific subjects like language, mathematics
2.	Social needs	Interaction with others, understanding of disability, adjustment with the environment
3.	Communication needs	Speech, written communication, learning grammar and usage of sentence, how to develop communication skills, use of equipment, etc.
4.	Mobility needs	To be able to move by oneself, familiarity with environment structure to facilitate mobility, training in obstacles identification.

(Contd.)

Sl.No..	*Types of needs*	*Curriculum adaptation*
5.	Living needs	Training in living independently and doing the daily routine tasks like bathing, wearing clothes, eating, managing home
6.	Vocational needs	Vocational needs of the children to be identified according to residual capacities, vocational training in schools with linkages of children with vocational training centers. Training for interviews, guidance for skills while meeting with employers.
7.	Safety needs	Use of apparatus, equipments and their maintenance, precautions for injuries
8.	Leisure needs	Identification of specific interests, aptitudes and abilities to be developed as leisure time activity like music, painting, crafts, playing, dramas, games, etc.
9.	Psychological needs	Understand and accept the child with his/her disability by self and others.

COMPONENTS OF CURRICULUM ADAPTATION

Curriculum adaptation has following components:

1. What to teach: The matter.
2. How to teach – the process and methodology.
3. Establishing learning environment.
4. Evaluation of teaching.

1. What to teach
   - Map entering behaviours of students
   - Setting goals of teaching
   - Task analysis (Breaking the task into small components)
   - Sequencing the tasks
   - Relating the tasks with real life situations

2. How to teach
   - Deciding Methodo-Logy
   - Plan Alterna-tives
   - Preparation of material
   - Sequencing the material
   - Pacing of Instruc-tions
   - Combining instructions with Practicals
   - Presenta-tion of instruction with Relevance

3. Establishment of Learning Environment

- Making Practice Learning and Interesting recapitulation
- Learning according to individual differences, needs of the Students
- Students friendly classroom management, seating, lighting, etc.
- all students participation
- Positive interaction among teacher & students, positive Communication
- keeping the students motivation intact

4. Monitoring and Evaluation

- Feedback on Learning
- Corrective measures/ modification in Instructions/material
- Measuring learning
- Extra-teaching for the needy

Strategy to Deal With Learning Disabled Child— a Summary

Learning Disabled	• Direct instruction material • Assignment preparation for practice of the topic • Use of examples • Simple content • Evaluation techniques to be modified • Identify the learning disability and curriculum adaptation accordingly • Training in time management • Training in peer interaction and relationship	• Direct instructions, extra instructions in skills where the child is weak • Repeated readings/writings • Use of calculators and other devices • Questions in simple language • Simple sentences • One task at a time • Make learning interesting • The length of the task should be reduced.

(B) CLASSROOM MANAGEMENT

The management of the classroom involves the identification of appropriate places for seating the learning disabled children, the arrangement of lighting system, ensuring adequate visibility of directions, locating apparatus and equipment at a proper place, etc. The children with disabilities should be given a seat where they can feel comfortable in seeing written material on the board and do not get disturbed from outside noise. A seat in the front of the class may be given so that teacher could help them in times of need. The peer group should be integrated to volunteer to help these children. The other children of the class should also be made aware of the various disabilities so that they could interact with the children with disabilities in a normal manner.

Wherever needed, interaction with parents should be had and they should be made partners in the development of the children. In Indian situations, parents and the community are not much aware of various disabilities and their coping strategies, and people are illiterate and biased about disabilities. In such situations it is more important that the school keeps the parents involved in the education process of the disabled child and apprises them of the problem and progress of these children.

Behaviour management is another aspect of class management. The desired behaviours should be developed through encouragement. The teacher should be sensitive to the problems of the children and should not pass derogatory comments. The teacher should also understand how and where to use the reinforcement for encouraging desired behaviours. He or she should consider ignoring undesired behaviours to the extent reasonable, and if such behaviours are not to be ignored should understand how to correct them by providing adequate directions.

(C) PEER TUTORING

In earlier days, academic non-achievement was considered as the responsibility of the child, but now, in modern times, the focus of blame for failure is shifting from student to the classroom, learning environment and the manner in which interaction between teacher and student and among students takes place. Various researches on classroom environment show that if good opportunities are created through proper learning atmosphere in the class, incidence of failures would be reduced. To create good learning environment in the class various techniques have been adopted, one of which being peer tutoring. In this technique, a student plays the role of a teacher and teaches the other students of his class or a student who is in the lower class. The teacher supervises such types of teaching.

The student-teacher learns the techniques of teaching, chooses a topic, prepares a lesson and then teaches other students. Such arrangement may be made while planning the weekly programme of teaching. Periods can be allotted to 'Peer Tutoring'.

Peer tutoring can be for one student or for a group of students or for the whole class. The student-teacher may take practice classes or teach the topics in which students face some difficulties to understand. Peer tutoring helps in a number of ways.

- The student-teacher develops self-confidence and a sense of responsibility.
- Before teaching the peers, he clears his own concepts relating to the topic he has to teach.
- Interaction among students develops, harmonious relations develop and dyslexic children are accepted in the class through this technique.
- Understanding with each other grows.
- The students who are finding difficulties in learning may clarify about their difficulties freely from the student—teacher, which they may not like to do in the regular class.
- Once better learning atmosphere is created through better interaction among students, undesirable behaviours from the students can be modified.

(D) TEACHING STRATEGIES

Becker and Armstrong said "a teacher can modify and control the behaviour of her students by controlling her under-response". In other words, a teacher can play a vital role in teaching of the learning disabled, if she can devise proper strategies of teaching. All children cannot be taught through one strategy or through one teaching module. The abilities of children vary, some learn fast while some are slow in understanding things. The understanding of various subjects also varies from student to student. Some children can understand the concepts of mathematics much faster than their counterparts, while others may be good in language skills. The teacher has to have a flexible approach to teaching. The teacher's role is not only to teach the subject but also to provide other training such as mobility training, self-care training, preparation of teaching material according to the needs of the disabled children, and so on.

(E) TEACHING AND SOCIAL PERCEPTION SKILLS

One of the objectives of teaching is modifying behaviours and motivating the child to learn new behaviours. The strategies of teaching should be adopted in such a manner that could lead to meet this objective of teaching. Behaviours that are viewed favourably in the society and are according to the accepted societal norms are to be learned. Such behaviours are developed through developing social skills. These skills are to be developed in the school so as to make a child good and respectable citizen of the society. Some of these social skills are:

- *Social competence skills:* These can help the disabled in dealing with others, making friends, respecting elderly, treating the needy with concern, making a place and acceptance in the society, showing desired behaviours etc.
- *Social Maintenance Skills:* These skills relate to helping other people in the society, accepting others with their problems, cooperate with others, learning to live with each other in the society and maintaining a social system.
- *Conflict Resolution Skills*: Conflicts take place in the society. How to deal with them? Teacher has to develop conflict resolution skills among the students. They are to be taught how to compromise and persuade others for conflict resolution. Good communication techniques help in conflict management.

  The above skills are to be developed in each child attending the school but for disabled children development of such skills is extremely necessary as they are to be taught to accept their disability also.

The social skills can be developed using various methods. These include:

(a) Direct intervention – Teacher can point out the behaviours that are not desirable.
(b) Direct teaching – Teacher can prepare direct instruction material to teach social skills.

(c) Indirect methods like demonstration, role-play, and modeling or showing films indicating desired behaviours etc.

UTILISATION OF RESOURCES

A. Choice of Instructional Material

Instructional material and methodology should be selected, which is culturally and traditionally appropriate and which the child could relate himself to. For example, children in Rajasthan may identify easily with puppets. Whenever new material is chosen, the child should be made fully familiar with it.

B. Management in the Class

The teacher has to perform various management functions in the class that involve planning, organising, controlling and motivating. For all these four functions, communication is extremely important. A teacher can plan the activities in the class, can organize according to the time schedule, control the class and motivate the students in learning if he knows the proper communication techniques. The teacher has to be positive, empathetic and patient. Verbal communications should follow the non-verbal communications. For example, if the teacher wants to appreciate a child it should also be reflected with the tone and pitch of the speech, the facial expressions and other body gestures. The teacher should be able to develop team spirit in the class and gaps between normal and disabled children should be reduced. Teacher should also have a flexible approach in dealing with disabled students. If a methodology of instruction is not giving the desired outcome, it should immediately be modified. Variety should also be introduced to make the teaching interesting.

In managing the behaviours of the students in a classroom,, alternative activities should be introduced. For example, if a student is hyper-active and trying to disturb the class, he may be given some constructive activity to be engaged in like writing an assignment or making a drawing or making a model with the clay. Such alternative activities can be introduced according to the need and topic of the period.

Disabled students should be encouraged to participate in the activities of the class. Assistance may be provided to facilitate their participation. In case the child has not picked up the activity correctly, he should be guided on how to do, through demonstration.

Class management also involves providing feedback on the behaviours and learning of the children and giving reinforcements. The teacher should be able to decide when and how to provide such feedback. In case of disabled children feedback should be given immediately. If the child is doing right, he should be encouraged, if he needs corrections, he should be stopped so that he may not practice a task in the wrong manner.

C. Parents Participation

Home is the first place where child interacts. Parents first observe the behaviours of a child and have first hand knowledge about the child. They know what interests the child, how he can be motivated, what are the triggers that make him aggressive or frustrated, what material or toys have been used to make him learn various activities etc. Thus, parents can play a very positive role in the development of the child if they share the information with the teacher in the school and other authorities. The school should plan regular interaction with the parents. In such meetings, progress of the child, the problem areas, the difficulties etc. should be discussed. In certain cases, parents should be apprised of the methods of dealing with their child. Parents may have to be provided training in dealing with their disabled child.

D. Community Resource Mapping

Community resources are helpful in the development of a disabled child. They can also help the child in learning his daily activities and also provide mobility training and develop functional skills. For example, if the disabled child is taken to a fruit shop, he can be trained—how to pick up fruits; how the fruits are kept in the shop; how and where to pay; and how to carry the purchased fruits back? Similarly, the child can be taken to other various places depending upon what is to be taught. He can, thus, be taught the use of stairs, elevators, use of parking places, use of other technological equipments, and familiarity with the area he has to live in. He can be taught how to keep himself safe and secure.

RESOURCES IN THE COMMUNITIES

For a disabled child, the following can be the resources:

1. Medical facilities like doctors, hospitals, and dispensaries.
2. Places of availability of equipments for the disabled.
3. Sheltered workshops.
4. Physiotherapists, speech therapists etc.
5. Hobby clubs, gyms, youth clubs, playgrounds.
6. The counselors.
7. The rehabilitation centers.
8. Market and other places of interests and functional areas like parks, museums.
9. Banks.
10. Libraries and computer centres.
11. Religious places.
12. Employment Exchange, placement agencies and employers.
13. NGOs that can help the disabled.
14. Other services available for the disabled like vocational training available at various places.

Schools should map these resources of the community a child lives in.

A child with learning disability finds it difficult to adjust with the school environment and learning even with appropriate intervention. All stakeholders, including the teachers, the parents and the peer group, have to support the child by encouraging and motivating. Parents should give quality time to the child and help him reading at home. They should also identify the specific ability of the child and provide opportunities to build self-confidence and high self-esteem. This is possible if the child has opportunities to develop his skills in the areas he can such as sports, hobbies, art, etc. It should be kept in mind that many known artists, athletes, scientists, suffered with learning disabilities.

A PRACTICAL APPROACH TO TEACH LEARNING DISABLED

1. *Use of Multi-senses:* children with learning disabilities learn better when they are taught in a manner where multi senses are

used. An example of multi-sensory teaching is where child is taught to see a word like 'cat'. It should be said by name and sound, and write it as well as show the picture of the cat

2. *Structured in Small Steps:* Lessons need to be highly structured. Structure should be based on small steps, with a proper sequence. Further learning should be based on what has been learnt earlier.

3. *Gradual Learning:* Skills are developed gradually. One skill is taught at a time. New things are taught only when the child has perfection on the old one.

4. *Practice*: Children with learning disabilities need regular revision.

5. *Learning with Activity:* Learning material should have clear objectives. A number of varying activities should be introduced to teach the subject.

6. *Learning and Utility:* Children need to understand the relevance and purpose of their lessons. They should be able to identify with the learning material. Learning should be related to their daily living.

7. *Teaching with Phonics:* Phonics is an educational technique that is often used to help teach, or improve, reading in children with dyslexia. In phonics, the emphasis is on sounds that the letters represent. For example, children are taught to see the connection between various words like rat, cat, sat, bat and the corresponding pattern of sounds.

8. *Self Reading:* Children should be encouraged to go for self reading. This independent reading provides confidence. They should read the books and material they like.

9. *Use of Computers-* Use of computers helps the learning disabled children. Word processing programmes are helpful as they have a spell-checker, and an auto-correct facility that can help highlight any mistakes in writing.

10. *Use of Colours:* In 1980, it was discovered that children with dyslexia could focus better on a page if a colour overlay was placed over it. Transparent colour overlays are available if the child complains that words seem fuzzy or 'dance about' when they are trying to read. Different children respond to different colours, so it is worth experimenting with a number of overlays in order to find the one that achieves the best result.

11. *Mastery Model*: This model was developed in India by National Council for Educational Research and Training (NCERT)

in 1983 with a view to avoid wastage of time, money and energies in the teaching-learning process. In this model, the responsibilities of learning have been shifted from the student to the teacher and school. The teacher has to ensure that students have mastery of all the concepts taught in the class. The model is a teaching process which involves presentation (cues), feedback (mastery testing) and correction (follow alternative approach) till the students learn and attain the desired level of mastery. The specific objectives of this model are:

- To help child learn at his own pace through a learning sequence.
- To enable students attain mastery over the learned concepts. In other words mastery of learning has to be demonstrated by the child.
- To enhance self-direction in learning.
- To develop problem-solving attitude through following a process.
- To enable students to make use of reference material.
- To develop analytical ability, reasoning and communication skills.

Assumptions: This model assumes that if appropriate material is used and desired time is given, students can learn and have mastery over the concepts. The assumptions in this model are:

1. Students can have mastery in learning if adequate time and practice is provided.
2. Students can work through sequential units in the subject if proper conditions of learning are created.
3. In the sequence of instructional units, students should not proceed to "second sequence till they have mastery over first unit.
4. Students' progress and feedback on the progress can make students learn.
5. Teacher and student interact in such a manner that learning takes place for both of them.
6. Mastery learning approach integrates students' needs with teaching programme.
7. Students can plan their own programme of study.

8. A flexible approach is necessary in term of instructions according to learner's ability.

The Model and its Sequencing: This model is implemented in four phases which are as follows:

Phase I: Phase I has four main activities: (a) Selecting content to be, taught, (b) Developing sequential teaching units, (c) Deciding goals in terms of mastery levels, (d) Teaching for learning the task.

All the subjects have various learning tasks which can be taught in various sequences. There is no single order or sequence that is perfect. Order, in most cases, can be modified according to the learner's needs and abilities of learning. On the other hand, there would be some subjects that can be taught only in one order as the second stage of learning would require learning at the first stage. In the Mastery Learning Model, the teacher has to divide a subject into different units in such a manner that learning of one unit is necessary for learning of second unit and so on. Relationship among various teaching units has to be worked out. These have to be interdependent. This is known as prerequisite learning for learning the next task. Core-teaching session can be had after every child attains the mastery over pre-requisite learning.

Phase II: Phase II relates to core teaching session. It has four components: (a) Clarity of instructional objectives, (b) Clarifying the expected mastery level, (c) Presenting learning tasks to the class, and (d) Measuring students' performance through unit tests.

It is evident that in core teaching session, the teacher teaches the whole class. Teaching objectives and expected performance from the students have to be told to the whole class. Instructions are to be imparted following any other model of teaching which a teacher considers appropriate such as Inquiry Teaching Model. After instructions, student's mastery level has to-be tested through a formative Test 1 (A number of formative tests can be prepared to be used during various phases of this model). On the feedback of the formative test, students can be divided into various groups according to their mastery level on the formative test. Differential teaching sessions can be held for various groups so formed.

The core teaching session should have behavioural objectives that have a sequence. The objectives should have following features:

- Objective should be directly related to exhibition of the students' mastery over a specific skill.

- The grouping of objectives should enable to develop relevant material of instructions.
- The grouping should help in diagnosis of students' achievements.
- Objectives should have serial dimension of abilities i.e. one ability should be a pre-requisite for the other.
- The sequence of objectives should be able to be grouped in sub-sequences or units.

Phase III: Phase III relates to the differential teaching sessions. In this of model following activities are to be conducted: (a) Grouping of students as per their achievements in the formative test, (b) Give alternative learning material to the students, (c) Small group interactions with peer teachers. (d) Organizing tutoring pairs where peer groups get involved. (e) Individual study plans, (f) Unit formative Test 2 and diagnosing students' difficulties. (g) Provide alternative learning material.

In this phase, Mastery groups of students are formed. One group would consist of those students who have achieved the mastery up to 80 to 100 per cent, known as M group. Another group would consist of those who have achieved a mastery level of 60 to 79 per cent. Both the groups would be of 4 to 5 students each. The students who have 60 to 79 per cent mastery level will need some additional material to read to go up to the higher mastery level. It in the form of self-study material.

The third group with an achievement of 40 to 60 per cent mastery would generally larger consisting of about 12 to 19 students. This larger group divided into two small groups and the members of M group can teach these groups (peer tutoring).

The remaining students would require teacher's attention. The teacher for this group has to change instructional strategy, instructional material and teaching technique and give formative Test 2 for evaluation of students. Those who will do not have mastery would require intensive teaching.

Phase IV: Fourth phase of the model relates to Intensive Teaching Session involving activities: (a) Tutoring by peers and teachers, (b) Giving material for practice. (c) Consolidation of achievements in various sessions. (d) Administering formative Test-3.

The students who remain outside the mastery level after Test 2 would form a smaller group as most of the students by this stage would have the requisite mastery over learning. This remaining group has to be given practice and drill and afterwards a Test 3. The children who still do not achieve desired of mastery must be helped outside the class by parents and teachers.

Teacher's Role

- Teacher is a manager of learning.
- He ensures that learning takes place according to the set objectives.
- He collects and prepares alternative learning material.
- He develops diagnostic tests.
- He sequences all the material.
- He has to set hierarchy of outcome.
- He forms groups of students according to mastery levels.
- He organizes individual study and work.
- He understands importance of interaction between him and students.
- He is a resource person, a selector, a diagnoser, a tutor and a responsible person.

His role in this model is very crucial.

Resources and Support Needed: To implement this model, a variety of resources and organizational support is needed:

- Mastery and diagnostic tests.
- Alternative material of instruction.
- Supplementary reading material.
- Reference material on the topic.
- Mindset to implement the model, giving additional time and unit formative evaluation.
- Flexibility of time scheduling and curriculum coverage.
- Individualized instruction material in terms of programme instructions, use of multi-media, etc.

Application of the Model: This Model can be applied in teaching subjects that can be sequenced, for example, teaching mathematics or grammar. Basic clarity of concepts can be taught using this model, as mastery over fundamentals would lead to effective learning at higher levels. Through this model one develops habit of self-learning and ability to consult reference material.

12. *Direct Instructions:* Direct instructions to the learning disabled have to be structured with scripted leasson plans. It should emphasize small learning at a time. Teacher should have frequent and continuous interaction with the child and correct the mistakes immediately made by him. Assessment of the progress has to be instant which may be different with that of the other students of the class. Assignments by the teacher can be planned as per the problems of child keeping in focus.

Innovations in Learning Disability

Specific interventions according to the child's specific problem can help a long way in improving the performance of the child. Although the learning disabilities are a life long problem, various types of interventions have been researched which had been helpful to deal with various learning disabilities up to a great extent.

Being a recent phenomenon, the issue of learning disabilities has got focus of social researches. More than 250 researches have identified social skill characteristics different among learning disabled with those of other children. Tanis Bryan is one of the pioneers also have conducted researches on the issue of social competence of learning disabled. He stated that differences were found in learning disabled and non-learning disabled children on quality of communication. Learning disabled children were less assertive, less persuable and less interactive.

Scientists are studying the functioning of the brain. They found out that neuroplasticity can come to the rescue of learning disorders. The term relates to the brain's ability to change to form new connections and generate new brain cells. This happens in response to the new experiences and learning that takes place in day to day life. Thus, neuroplasticity can help in retraining of the brain. Once it is established that the brain can change, the learning disabilities relating to brain disorders can be tackled with new hope. The concept of neuroplasticity works like a telephone, as the faults in the connecting lines of the telephone can effect the telephone communication. It gets repaired if new line is laid. Similarly, learning disability can get repaired with new neural connections.

As has been stated earlier, earlier detection and timely intervention can provide very positive results in learning disabled. But generally severity of the problem is not detectable. National Institute of Mentally Handicapped under Ministry of Social Justice and Empowerment has developed Indian Scale for Assessment of Autism (ISAA) which is a new screening tool. This may be available soon for use.

In another research a nasal spray containing 'oxytocin' has been found to be effective for autistic children who find it difficult to communicate and socialize with others. It is said that this spray helps and impedes these skills. Such researches are in their infancy but future for learning disabled is bright with these continued efforts of researchers, governments and other stakeholders.

Annexure I
List of Persons and Organisations Helping Disabled

1. Jayanti Narayan
   Dept of Special Education
   National Instititute for the
   MentallyHandicapped
   Manovikas Nagar PO
   Secunderabad 500003.
2. Dr. Sudheer Reddy
   Dept. of Education
   Osmania University
   Huyderabad
3. Lakshmi Narsimhan
   Help child Charitable
   Educational Trust
   B-78, Indian Airlines Colony,
   Begumpet
   Secunderabad 500003
4. Dept. of child phychiarty
   NIMHANS, Bangalore, 560029
5. Dr. Joe Rozario
   290 / 7, Venkataramaiah
   Layout, Ramamurty Nagar
   Banaswadi, Bangalore
   560043.
6. Rukmini Krishnaswamy
   31, 5th Cross, Off 5th Main,
   Indira Nagar Stage I
   Bangalore 560038
7. Shonali Arulmani
   Promise Foundation
   15, Infantry Road
   Bangalore 560001
8. Reena Sen
   Spastics Society of Eastern
   India
   P-35/1 Taratolla Road
   Calcutta 700007.
9. Purobi Bose
   Reach — Society for Remedial
   Education
   Uday Sankar Sarani
   Golf Green Calcutta 700045.
10. Nirmala Pandit
    Madras Dyslexia Association
    10/1, Sambasivan Street
    T. Nagar Chennai 600017.
11. Lalitha Ramanujan
    Alpha to Omega Learning
    Centre, 12, Gajapathy Road
    Kilpauk Chennai 600010
12. Usha Ramakrishnan
    Spastics Society of India
    No. 1. Ranjith Road,
    Kotturpuram Chennai
    600085.
13. Dr. M.C. Mathew
    Ashirwad Child
    Development
    and Research Centre
    AD-80, 5th Avenue,
    Anna Nagar Chennai 600040.
15. T. Geetha
    Dept of Special Education
    Avinashiligam Deemed
    University, Coimbatore 641043.
16. Ranjini Krishnamurthy
    Vidya Niketan, No 5 /10 B
    Puliakulam Road
    Coimbatore 641045.
17. Sunita Sodhi
    Educare Charitable Trust
    M-2, Hauz Khas
    New Delhi 110048.
18. National Open School
    (Dept of Education)
    B, 31 B, Kailash Colony
    New Delhi 110016.

19. Onita Nakra
Special Education Centre
D 6/1 Vasant Vihar
New Delhi 110057.
20. Maharaji Swami Mansigh
Vidyalaya
Swami Rarn Singh Road
Jaipur 302004.
21. Dr. N.R. Arun Kishore
Venuviharam
Sankarayya Road
Thrissur 681004.
22. Priyo Lal 5, Nemi Road
Dehradun 248001
23. Vimala Venkatesan
Guidance Centre
Karnal 132001.
24. Bonni—Belle Pickard
Music Dept.
Kodaikanal Internationl
School
Kodaikannal 624101.
25. Dr. S. Ramaa
Dept. of Special Education
Regional college of Education
Mysore 570006.
26. Dr. Tapati Dutta
Dept of Special Education
Regional Institure of
Education
Bhubaneswar 751007.
27. Child care centre
Gandhi Nagar
Kochi 682020.
28. Raksha Institute of Special
Education
XIV / 185, First floor
Chapel Road, Chullickal
Kochi 682005
29. Dr. Smrithi Swarup
Dept. of special Education
SNDT Women's Uiniversity
Sir Vithaldas Vidya Vihar
Juhu Road
Santa Cruz (W) Mumbai
400049.
30. Vinita Pandit
Mharashtra Dyslexia
Association
303, Jharna, Dr. Ambedkar
Road
Khar (West) Mumbai 400052.
31. Nindu Patni
Vidya Jyoti School for Slow
Learners
904, Amrai Camp, Off
Bandarkar Road
Pune 411004.
32. Lavina Choudari
Vardhin, Centre for Special
Education, 885/2, Bandarkar
Road Pune 411004.
33. Aalam
JB-35B Janta Flat, Hari Nagar, New Delhi-110064; Phone: 2549 9229 Focus Area: Multiple disability; weaker section of society.
34. Aanchal School
Aanchal School, Kautilya Marg, New Delhi-110021; Phone: 2301 4165 Focus Area: Mentally retarded.
35. Aasha Kiran
Avantika Complex, Rohini Sector 1, New Delhi-1 10085 Phone: 2716 0142, 2727 2760 Fax: 2727 2191 Focus Area: Mentally ill.
36. Aashray Adhikar Abhiyan
E-270 Greater Kailash Part II, New Delhi 110048; Phone: 26418885 7 e-mail: righttoshelter@hotmail.com Focus Area: Children, women, elderly, disabled and destitute.

37. Abhilasha Special Education Center
E-24B MIG Flat (DDA), G-8 Area, Mayapuri, New Delhi-110027; Phone: 25143123 Focus Area: Mentally ill; Hearing impaired; Speech disorder.
38. Action for Autism
Sector 5 Jasola Vihar, Behind Sai Niketan New Delhi 110025 Tel: 91 11 65347422,40540991/92 actionforautism@gmail.com Website: http://www.autism india.org Focus Area: A Premier center for Standard Therapy of Autism and Learning disabilities.
39. ADP—North Delhi /a Project of World Vision India)
A-4244, Manushree Building, Commercial Complex; Dr.Mukherji Nagar, New Delhi; Phone: 27651924 e-mail: adprd@ndf.vsnl.net.in Focus Area: Orthopaedically handi-capped.
40. Advanced Medical Rehab Clinic (AMRC) J-222, at Sarita Vihar, New Delhi-110076, Phone: 41403344 (Centers also at Faridabad, Munirka, Dwarka); Focus Area: cerebral palsy, autism, polio rehabilitation and other causes of locomotor and multiple disability
Contact person: Dr. Ajay Gupta, Mobile: 9810692375, Website: www.rehabclinic.co.in; Email: info@rehabclinic.co.in
41. Akshaya Pratishthan
Sector D Pocket III Vasant Kunj, New Delhi-110070; Phone: 26132565, 26124923; Fax: 26896143 Focus Area: Orthopaedically disabled; Locomotor disabled; Mentally ill.
42. Ali Yavar Jung National Institute for the Hearing Handicapped
Norfhern Regional Centre, Kasturba Niketan Complex, Lajpat Nagar II, New Delhi-110024; Phone: 26835093 Focus Area: Hearing Impaired; Speech impaired.
43. All India Confederation of the Blind
Braille Bhawan, Near Rajiv Gandhi Cancer Hospital, Sector 5, Rohini, New Delhi-110085; Phone: 27054082, 27247469; Fax: 27050915; e-mail: aicb@mailcity.com Focus Area: Visually impaired.
44. ADP—South Delhi (a Project of World Vision)
I-38 First Floor, Lajpat Nagar-Il, New Delhi-110024; Phone: 26928695 Focus: Orthopae-dically handicapped, over all, community development.
45. All India Deaf and Dumb Society
Plot no. 487, Institutional Area, Karkari More, Near Preet Vihar, Vikas Marg, New Delhi-110092 Phone: 22156670, 22414224 Focus Area: Hearing impaired.
46. All India Federation of the Deaf (refer to serial no.14) 18, Northend Complex, RK Ashram Marg, New Delhi-1 10001; Phone: 2336 4766 Focus Area: Hearing impaired.
47. All India Federation of the Deaf, Training Center (refer to

serial no. 13) 12-13, Institutional area, Shaheed Jit Singh Marg, New Delhi-110016; Phone: 26563984, 26966683 Focus Area: Hearing impaired.

48. World Vision India (Refer to serial no. 7 and 11) B-3 Lajpat Nagar-II, New Delhi-1 1024 Phone: 26831168 Focus Area: Overall community development.
49. All India Sports Council of the Deaf
    8, Northend Complex, RK Ashram Marg, New Delhi 110401; Phone: 2336462.4 Focus Area: Hearing impaired; Speech problem.
50. Amar Jyoti Research and Rehabilitation Center
    Karkardooma, Vikas Marg, New Delhi-110092 Phone: 22151286 Fax: 22154936 e-mail: amarjyoti@del2.vsnl.net.in Focus Area: Multiple disability.
51. Andh Maha Vidyalaya
    Panch Kuin Road, New Delhi-110001; Phone: 23364209 Focus Area: Visually impaired
52. Asha Awwa School for Handicapped Children
    Base Hospital; Delhi Cantonment, New Delhi; Phone: 25691997 Focus Area: Mentally retarded and hearing impaired (age group 5-14 years).
53. Ashray (Association for Social Health & Rehabilitation Action by Youth)
    Basti Vikas Kendra, Tagore Road, Kamla Market, New Delhi-110002; Phone: 23232377 Focus Area: Multiple disability.
54. Association for the Development of Multiple Handicapped Children
    B-56, Defence Colony, New Delhi-110024 Phone: 24623548 Focus Area: Multiple disabilities; Cerebral palsy; Post polio residual paralysis; Mental retardation.
55. Asra [Action for Self Reliance and Alternative)
    WZ-14A, Jeet Shopping Market Budhela, Vikas Puri, New Delhi-110018; Phone: 25526844 Focus Area: Orthopaedically handicapped.
56. Association for Advancement & Rehabilitation of Handicapped (Aaroh)
    224, Vasant Enclave, New Delhi-110057; Phone: 26144721 Fax: 26144721 Focus Area: Mentally ill.
57. Association of the National Brotherhood for Social Welfare
    21-22, New Rohtak Road, Karol Bagh, New Delhi-1 10005; Phone: 23628641 Fax: 23520405 Focus Area: Orthopaedically handicapped; Mentally ill.
58. Astha (Alternative Strategies for the Handicapped)
    S-268, Greater Kailash II, New Delhi-1 10048; Phone: 26419862 Focus Area: Multiple disability.
59. AWAAZ (branch office) (refer below)
    Block OI, plot no 71 A, Budh Vihar, New Delhi-110015; Phone: 2727 6295
60. Awaaz Special School (refer to serial no. 26) K-87, Kirti Nagar, New Delhi-110015; Phone:

25451301, 27276295 Focus Area: Hearing impai-red; Mentally retarded.

61. Balvantray Mehta Vidya Bhawan—Anguridevi Sher Singh Memorial Academy
Block E, G, & H Masjid Moth, Greater Kailash II, New Delhi-1 10048; Phone: 26441798, 26288815 Focus Area: Mentally ill
62. Bhagwan Mahaveer Vikas Sahayata Samiti
L-43, Connaught Circus, New Delhi-110001; Phone: 23323350, 25785133 Focus Area: Physically handicapped.
63. Bharat Blind School
510 A Circular Road, Shohdra, New Delhi-110032; Phone: 22423021 Focus Area: Visually impaired.
64. Bharat Blind Technical Welfare Society
Central Market, Madangir, New Delhi-1 10067; Phone: 26983520 Focus Area: Visualiy impaired.
65. Bharatiya Vidya Bhavan Kasturba Gandhi Marg, New Delhi-110001; Phone: 23389943, 23384881 Focus Area: Slow Learner.
66. Bhartiya Blind Educational Cultural Welfare
SOCIETY 61 / 1-B-1 1, Telewara, Shahdara, New Delhi-1 10032; Phone: 2222 8016, 2216 7375 Focus Area: Visually impaired.
67. Blind Relief Association
Lal Bahadur Shastri Marg, Near Hotel Oberoi, New Delhi-1 10003; Phone: 24361376; Fax: 24364730
e-mail: lbsbra@delhi1.mtnl.net.in Focus Area: Visually impai-red.
68. Carenidhi [Centre for Applied Research and Education on Neuro-developmental Impairments and Disability—Related Health Initiatives) C-II/10, Ansari Nagar, A.I.I.M.S. Campus, N.Delhi-110029; Phone: 26857755 Fax: 26167459 E-mail: carenidhi@hotmail.com Focus Area: Multiple disability.
69. Child Guidance Center
Department of Social Work (Delhi Univ.), 3 University Road, New Delhi-1 10009; Phone: 2725 7881 Focus Area: Multiple disability; Mentally ill; Behavioural problems; Learning disability.
70. Child Guidance Center
National Institute of Public Co-Operation & Child Development, 5, Siri Institutional Area, Hauz Khas, New Delhi-110016; Phone: 2696 3002/ 3204/ 3378 Focus Area: Multiple disability; Speech problem; Slow learners in the age groups 0-14; Scholastic problems.
71. Child Guidance Center
Zakir Hussain Memorial Welfare Society, Jamia Millia Islamia (T T T), New Delhi-110025; Phone: 26842554 (R), 26843909 Focus Area: Mentally ill; Behavioural and speech problems; Educational problems.
72. Child Guidance Center
RAK College of Nursing,

Lajpat Nagar, New Delhi-110024; Phone: 2643 6668 Focus Area: Mental disability; Psychological problems; Communication disorders.

73. Child Guidance Center
Dr. Z.H. Memorial Welfare Soc., Jamia Sr. Sec. School Camps, Jamia Nagar, N Delhi-25; Phone: 26843909 Focus Area: Multiple disability.

74. Child Guidance Clinic
Kalawati Saran Children's Hospital, Bangla Sahib Marg, New Delhi-110025; Phone: 23735090 Focus Area: Multipie disability; Mentally ill; Physical and emotional problems.

75. Child Guidance Clinic
Department of Psychiatry AIIMS, New Delhi-110029; Phone: 26594412 Focus Area: Mentally ill; Slow learners; Psychological disorders.

76. Concerned Action now (Can)
B-IV, 3067 Aruna Asaf Ali Road, Vasant Kunj,, New Delhi-110070; Phone: 26132815, 26122705 Fax: 26104865 E-mail: baquer@ del2.vsnl.net.in, Website: www.indev.nic.in/can Focus Area: All disabilities.

77. Cripple—Aid—Trust
6-B MIG Flats, Shivam Enclave, Jhilmil, New Delhi-110032; Phone: 22202085 Fax: 22445066 Focus Area: Multiple disability

78. Deaf and dumb Co-operative Industrial Society Ltd.
Plot No 7, Weavers Col~ony, Bharat Nagar, New Delhi 110052; Phone: 27233320 Focus Area: Hearing impaired.

79. Delhi Bharat Vikas Foundation
113A Pocket B, Dilshad Garden, New Delhi 110095; Phone: 22296387, 22120559 Focus Area: Physically handicapped.

80. Delhi Association of the Deaf
92, Kamla Market, New Delhi-110002; Phone: 23233991, 23235065, 23236521 Fax: 23230147 Focus Area: Hearing impaired (age group 5-28 years.

81. Delhi Brotherhood Society
Brotherhood House, 7, Court Lane, New Delhi-1 10054; Phone: 23931432, 24626309 Fax: 23981025 e-mail: mono@del2.vsnl.net.in Focus Area: Orthopaedically disabled.

82. Delhi Cheshire Home
Delhi Cheshire House, Opp. Holy Family Hospital, Okhla Road, New Delhi-25; Phone: 26311069, 26917560 Focus Area: Orthopaedically Handicapped; Mentally retarded.

83. Delhi Foundation of Deaf Women
DDA Community Hall, Gali Chandiwali Paharganj, New Delhi-110055; Phone: 23533276 Focus Area: Hearing impaired women in age group 16 years and above.

84. Delhi Foundation of Deaf Women
DDA Community Centre 1 st floor, Chandiwali Gali, Paharganj, New Delhi; Phone: 23533276 Focus Area: Hearing impaired (women of 1 8 and above).

85. Delhi Society for the Welfare of Mentally Retarded Children
Okhla Centre, Okhla Marg,

opposite Holy Family Hospital, New Delhi-1 10025; Phone: 26310979 Focus Area: Mentally ill.

86. Delhi Sports Council for the Deaf
J-l0 Saket, New Delhi-110017; Phone: 26527303 Focus Area: Hearing impaired.
87. Department of Psychiatry
Dr. Ram Manohar Lohia Hospital, Park Street, New Delhi-110001; Phone: 2336 5525/363 Focus Area: Multiple disability; Mentally ill, Orthopaedically handicapped.
88. Department of Social Welfare
l, Canning lane, K.G. Marg, New Delhi; Phone: 2338 2687, 23384904 Fax: 23388813 Contact Person: Nisha Agrawal, PRO Focus Area: Mentally retarded; Visually impaired; Hearing impaired.
89. Family of Disabled (Fod)
Bl/500, Janakpuri, New Delhi-1 10058; Phone: 2559 7328 Fax: 2550 2502
e-mail: foddelhi@yahoo.com Focus Area: Multiple disability.
90. Federation for the Welfare of Mentally Retarded
Shaheed Jeet Singh Marg, Special Institutional Area, New Delhi -110067; Phone: 26513432 Fax: 26862158 Focus Area: Mentally retarded.
91. Genetic and Mental Retardation Clinic
Dept. of Paediatrics, AIIMS, New Delhi-1 10029; Phone: 26561123 Contact Person: Prof. lshwar C Verma Focus Area: Multiple disability; Genetic and birth defects.
92. Government Lady Noyce Secondary School for the Deaf
Kotla Feroz Shah, New Delhi-110002; Phone: 23319419 Focus Area: Hearing impaired.
93. Government Model Senior Secondary School-2
Ludlow Castle, 5, Shyam Nath Marg, New Delhi-1 10054; Phone: 23966853 Focus Area: Mutiple disability; Hearing impaired; Physical disability; Mental disability in the age groups of 5-18 Years.
94. Government Secondary School for Blind Boys
Kingsway Camp, New Delhi-110009; Phone: 23535575, 23555044 Focus Area: Visually impaired.
95. Handicapped Welfare Federation
14 (LF), Tansen Marg, New Delhi-1 10001; Phone: 23710791, 23328730 Focus Area: Locomotor disability.
96. Handicapped Women's Welfare Association
BB 5A, DDA Flats, Shalimar Bagh, New Delhi; Phone: 27263218, 27263451 Focus Area: Multiple disability in women and children in the age groups 3-40 Years; Hearing impaired; Mentally ill; Orthopaedically handicapped.
97. Handicapped Women's Welfare Association School for the Handicapped
Sector-14, Madhuban Chowk, Near Tibet Hostel, Rohini, New Delhi-1 10085 Phone: 2726 3218, 27263451 Focus Area: Orthopaedically handicapped; Hearing impaired; Mentally ill.

98. Hemophilia Society (Delhi) Lions Hospital and Research Centre Premises, Khizrabad, New Friends Colony, N. Delhi 65; Phone: 26929281 Focus Area: Hemophilia
99. Hemophilia Federation (India) A-128 Mohammadpur, behind Bhikaji Cama Place, New Delhi-110066; Phone: 26175791, 26174020 Focus Area: Hemophilia.
100. Hind Kusht Nivaran Sangh 33-34, North End Complex, Panchkuian Road Crossing, R.K. Ashram Marg, New Delhi-1, Phone: 23364639 Focus Area: leprosy
101. Hope Foundation D-32, First floor, Jangpura Extension, New Delhi-110014; Phone: 24317359, 24314130, 24313047 e-mail: ravisharma@hopeww.org; Website: www.HOPEWW.org Focus Area: Leprosy; Women and child.
102. Indcare [Integrated nat. dev. Center for Advancement, Reform & Education) 1030, Vikas Kunj, New Delhi-110018; Phone: 25531031, 25623664 Fax: 25531031 e-mail: indcare@bol.net.in Focus Area: Women, Aged disabled; Children.
103. India Vision Foundation 2, Talkatora Lane, New Delhi-110001; Phone: 23792961 Fax: 23792928 e-mail: ivfindia@vsnl.com Focus Area: Physical disability; Visually impaired; Mentally ill; Hearing impaired.
104. Inspiration AG1 123D, Vikaspuri, New Delhi-110018; Phone: 25611861, 25412463 Focus Area: Mentally ill; Multiple disability; Autistic, Spastic.
105. Institution for the Blind Amar Colony, lajpat Nagar IV, New Delhi-110024; Phone: 26411915, 26216506 Focus Area: Visually impaired boys.
106. Institution for the Biind [Andh Vidyalaya) Panchkuin Road, New Delhi-110001; Phone: 23364265 Focus Area: Visually impaired boys.
107. Ishwar P8-B Hauz Khas Enclave, New Delhi-110016. India. Phones: 26568624, 26855154, 9810269298, 9810075122 Email: ishwar.ngo@indiatimes.com; Web: www.ishwar-ngo.org Focus Area: Developmental activities with primary focus on children and young adults having any form of disability. Sports programme for 'differently—abled' children, like cricket, basketball, swimming, skating, karate and chess, under the guidance of trained sports coaches and therapists.
108. Jan Madhyam 148 Zamrudpur, New Delhi-110048; Phone: 26473525 Fax: 26473525 e-mail: jmadhayam@yahoo.com Focus Area: Multiple disability; learning disabilities; Intellectual disabilities.
109. Janta Adarsh Andh Vidyalaya Siri Fort Road, Behind bungalow No. 4, Sadiq Nagar, New Delhi-110049; Phone: 26250701, 26250702 Focus Area: Visually impaired.

110. Jeevan Jyoti Missionaries of Charity
Near Bhogal, opp Ganga Automobiles, Jangpura, New Delhi Focus Area: Mentally ill; Orthopaedically handicapped.
111. Mahalakshmi Udyog Shala
R-23, Shri Mahalakshmi Udyogshala, East Vinod Nagar, near Mayur Vihar, N. Delhi-110091; Phone: 22475609 Focus Area: Disabled persons who are able to work on machines.
112. Manovikas Kendra
Kulachi Hansraj Model School, Ashok Vihar Phase I, New Delhi-110052; Phone: 27124498 Focus Area: Multiple disability.
113. Maximizing Employment to Serve the Handicapped (Mesh)
Shop no 5, Local Shopping Center, Uday Park, New Delhi 110049; Phone: 26568048, 26965039
E-mail: mesh@del6.vsnl.net.in
Website: www.mesh.org.in
Focus Area: Providing opportunities for social and economic development to disabled and leprosy—affected people. Contact person: Mrs.Jacqueline Bonney, Tel. 011-26568048
114. Ministry of Social Justice and Empowerment, Govt. of India
Shastri Bhawan 6th Floor, New Delhi 110001
115. Model School for Mentally Deficient Children
Kasturba Niketan, Lajpat Nagar, New Delhi-110024; Phone: 26834328 Fax: 26831012 Focus Area: Mentally retarded.
116. Multipurpose Training Center for the Deaf
AIFD, 12-13 Institutional Area, Shahid Jeet Singh Marg, New Delhi-110067; Phone: 26563984 Focus Area: Hearing impaired.
117. Muni Shri Roop Chandra Naturopathy and Acupuncture Centre (M.S.R.)
Jain Ashram, Opp. Sarai Kale Khan Bus Terminal, P.O. Box No. 3240, N. Delhi-110013; Phone: 26821348 Focus Area: Special treatment for specific diseases.
118. Muskaan — Parents Assoc. for the Welfare of Children with Mental Handicap
A-28, Hauz Khas, New Delhi-110016; Phone: 26566766 Focus Area: Mentally handicapped.
119. Nursery Primary School for the Deaf
Kingsway Camp, Seva Kutir Complex, New Delhi-110009; Phone: 27465731 Focus Area: Hearing impaired.
120. National Blind Youth Association
C, G.H.S, Complex, Fazalpur Mandawali, near Patparganj Depot, New Delhi-110092; Phone: 22460502 Focus Area: Visually impaired.
121. National Federation of the Blind
2721, Chowk Sangtrashan, Pahar Ganj, New Delhi-110055; Phone: 23550277, 23971901 Fax: 32556789 Focus Area: Visually impaired
122. National Institute for Mentally Handicapped
Regional Training Centre (North), Lajpat Nagar, New Delhi; Phone: 26820643 Fax:

26831012 Focus Area:Mentally ill; Orthopaedically handicapped.

123. National Institute for Mentally Handicapped (Nimh)
Model School, Kasturba Niketan, Lajpat Nagar II, New Delhi-110024; Phone: 26820643 /4328 Fax: 26831012 Focus Area: Mentally handicapped.

124. Nav Jyoti Centre
B-1l, Vasant Kunj, New Delhi-110070; Phone: 26144721, 26899044 Focus Area: Mentally ill.

125. Navkiran School
91, Kiran Vihar, Near K D Hospital, New Delhi-110092; Phone: 22226732 Focus Area: Mentally ill; Speech disorder.

126. Ncpedp (National Center for Promotion of Employment for Disabled Persons)
25, Yusuf Sarai, Green Park Extension, New Delhi-110016; Phone: 26854306, 26967910, e-mail: ncped@nde.vsnl.net.in Focus Area: Multiple disability.

127. New Delhi Young Men's Christian Association
Jai Singh Road, New Delhi 110001; Phone: 23746036, 23746034, 23361915; Fax: 23746035, 23746032 Focus Area: Mentally ill children; Development of community.

128. Occupational Therapy Home for Children
109, Press Road, New Delhi-110002; Phone: 23239930, 23237262 Focus Area: Orthopaedically handicapped; Mentally ill.

129. Oubure (Org. For Ubiquitous Backward Uplifting Research and Education)
D28 Shastri Nagar, Hapur Road, Ghaziabad-201002; Phone: 914 755716 Focus Area: All disabilities.

130. Parivaar — a Federation of Parent Associations
A-2520, Netaji Nagar, New Delhi-100023; Phone: 26870987, 23311711, 23318329 Fax: 23316674
e-mail: jagdishmehta@hotmail.com Focus Area: Multiple disability.

131. Parmath Misslon Hospital
23/7, Shakti Nagar, New Delhi-110007; Phone: 27244300, 27246595 Fax: 27213798 Focus Area: Orthopaedically handicapped.

132. Pawan
NDMC, Kautilya Marg, Chanakyapuri, New Delhi 110021; Phone: 23014165 Focus Area: Hearing impaired.

133. Perfect Foundation School
R2-26P/9 Indira Park, Palam Colony, New Delhi-110045; Phone: 25415647, 25036586 Focus Area: Orthopaedically handicapped.

134. Prakash Deep Educational & Vocational Society
1 /5308-A, Street no 13, Balbir Nagar Extension, Shahdara, New Delhi-110032; Phone: 22174003 Focus Area: Multiple disability.

135. Pramila Bai Chauhan Mook Badhir Vidyalay
487, Institutional Area, Karkari More, New Delhi-110032;

Phone: 22206670, 22156670
Focus Area: Hearing impaired.

136. Prateek— an Instutute for Children with Special Needs
Address: H-125, Kunwar Singh Nagar, Budah Bazar Road, Nilothi More, Nangloi, New Delhi-110041 011-65195257, 9891492177;
Contact Person: Mr. Amit Kumar, e-mail-personincharge @yahoo.com
Focus Area: Multiple Disability, Weaker Section Of Society
137. Raghudev Memorial School of Vocational Studies 9 Rajpur Road, Civil Lines, Delhi; Phone: 23555324 e-mail: mpuri@vsnl.com Focus Area: Mentally retarded in the age group 16 and above.
138. Rajiv Gandhi Foundation
Jawahar Bhawan, Dr. Rajendra Prasad Road, New Delhi-110001; Phone: 23755117, 23755118 Fax: 23755119
e-mail: dpw@rgfindia.com
Focus Area: Multiple disability.
139. Rajkumari Amrit Kaur Child Study Centre
Dept. Of Child Development, Lady Irwin College, Sikandara Road, New Delhi-110001; Phone: 23719859 Focus Area: Orthopaedically handicapped; Mentally ill; Visually impaired; Partially hearing impaired; Behavioural problems; Multiple disability; Autism; Cerebral palsy.
140. Rashtriya Virjanand Andh Kanya Vidyalaya Society
M-19 Lajpat Nagar, New Delhi-110024; Phone: 26310465
Focus Area: Visually impaired girls.
141. Rashtriya Virjanand Andh Kanya Vidyalay Society
New Rajinder Nagar, Shankar Road, New Delhi-110060; Phone: 25781370, 25746002
Focus Area: Visually impaired girls.
142. Rehabilitation Unit in Audio Logy & Speech Pathology Department of ENT, AIIMS, New Delhi-110029; Phone: 26561123
Focus Area: Mentally ill; Speech and language problems; Voice disorder.
143. Sadhu Vaswani International School Girls
2nd Street, Shanti Niketan, New Delhi; Phone: 24670242, 26872390 Focus Area: Slow learner.
144. Sahara Manovikash Kendra: A Project of Janseva Education Society
RP Block, Pitam Pura, New Delhi-110034; Phone: 27224075
Focus Area: Mentally ill; Orthopaedically handicapped; Speech disorder; Hearing impaired.
145. Sahas Society for the Welfare of Mentally Handicapped
Sector III, Type III, 190, Sadiq Nagar, New Delhi-110049; Phone: 26259531 Focus Area: Mentally ill.
146. Saini Speech and Hearing Clinic
3097, Street Tara Chand, Darya Ganj (Behind Golcha), New Delhi-110002; Cable: 23270864
Focus Area: Mentally retarded; Spastics; Autism.

147. Samadhan
F-Block Main Park, Sector 5, Dakshinpuri, New Delhi-110062; Phone: 26974367 Fax: 26863625
e-mail: samadhan@del3.vsnl.net.in;
Web site: www.indiasocial.org/samadhan
Focus Area: Mentally retarded; Slow learner.
148. Samarth the Professionals
B-58, Tagore Garden Extension, New Delhi-110027; Phone: 25193726, 27294094 Fax: 25163106 Focus Area: Children (underprivileged).
149. Sankaras Vidya Kendra
Paschimi Marg, Vasant Vihar, New Delhi 110057
Focus Area: Mentally retarded
150. Sanjivini Society for Mental Health
A-b, Satsang Vihar Marg, Qutub Institutional Area, (south of IIT), New Delhi-110067; Phone: 26862222/4488 Web page: www.indiasocial.org/sanjivini Focus Area: Emotional problems; Behavioural disorder.
151. Sapna
139, Asiad Village, New Delhi-110049 Focus Area: Orthopaedically handicapped; Hearing impaired; Speech problems.
152. School for Mentally Retarded Children
Campus of Government Lady Noyce School, behind Ambedkar Stadium, Delhi Gate, N. Delhi; Phone: 23720247 Focus Area: Mentally retarded
153. Society for Child Development — Prabhaat School
B-930, Shashtri Nagar, New Delhi-110052; Phone: 23555324 Focus Area: Mentally ill; Slow learner
154. Society for Child Development
10/15, Shakti Nagar, New Delhi-110007; Phone: 23923559 119. Society For Friendship Education And Development (SOFED) H. No. 80-B, Street 7, Zakir Nagar, P.O. Jamia Nagar, New Delhi-110025; Phone: 26312105 Focus Area: Multiple disability.
155. Society for Rehabilitation & Research of the Handicapped
Swami Shivananda Bhawan, Amar Colony, Llajpat Nagar IV, New Delhi-110024; Phone: 26420697 Focus Area: Hearing impaired.
156. Spastics Society of Northern India (SSNI)
2, Balbir Saxena Marg, Hauz Khas, New Delhi; Phone: 26569107, 26864714
e-mail: ssni@vsnl.net.in Focus Area: Cerebral palsy; Neuro—muscular disorders; Multiple disability.
157. Special Center, See Also Nimh
C/o. CASP PLAN Project, 8/1780, A Govindpuri Exten., N. Delhi-110019; Phone: 26460893 Fax: 26478213 Focus Area: Mentally ill.
158. ST. Thomas Girls Senior Secondary Mandir Marg, New Delhi-110001; Phone: 23364094 Focus Area: Slow learner

159. Suniye
60 Feet Road Corner, 1 /4992 loni Road, Shahdara, New Delhi-110032; Phone: 22111817 Fax: 22291817 Focus Area: Hearing impaired children.

160. Tamana Association
D-6 Street, Vasant Vihar, New Delhi-110057; Phone: 26143853, 26148269 Fax: 26143853 Focus Area: Mentally handicapped; Down's Syndrome, Autism.

161. Thalassemics India
C-1 /59 Safdarjung Development Area, New Delhi 110016; Phone: 26499666 Fax: 26855721, 26495300 e-mail: thalind@ndf.vsnl.net.in Focus Area: Thalassemia

162. The Eciat Society for Mentally Retarded
I-3/127, Sector 16 Rohini, New Delhi-110085; Phone: 27295838, 27262489, 27264920 Fax: 27882847 Focus Area: Mentally ill.

163. The Educare Charitable Trust [Regd)
M-2, Hauz Khas, New Delhi-110016; Phone: 26565061, 26857560 e-mail: sunitasodhi@hotmail.com Focus Area: Dyslexia; Attention deficit disorder; Learning disorders.

164. The Enabling Center
Lady Irwin College, Sikandra Road, New Delhi-110001; Phone: 23274411 Focus Area: Multiple disability; Visually or Hearing Impaired; Cerebral palsy; Autism; Mentally retarded.

165. The Institute for the Physically Handicapped (Ministry of Social Justice & Empowerment, Govt. of India)
4, Vishnu Digamber Marg, New Delhi-110002 Focus Area: Orthopaedically handicapped.

166. The Leprosy Mission [India]
CNI Bhavan, 16 Pandit Pant Marg, New Delhi-110001; Phone:23718261, 23716920 Fax: 23710803
e-mail: tlmindia@del2.vsnl.net.in Focus Area: Leprosy

167. The National Association for the Blind
Sector V, R.K. Puram, New Delhi-110022; Phone: 26175886, 26176379 Fax: 26187650
e-mail: nabdelhi@del2.vsnl.net.in Focus Area: Visually impaired; Multiple disability.

168. Training Cum Production Center
20, North Avenue, Punjabi Bagh, New Delhi-110026; Phone: 25412871 Focus Area: Mentally ill; Orthopaedically handicapped.

169. Training—Cum—Earning Center for Handicapped Women of Weaker Section
Institute No. 1, Institutional Zone, Hudson Lines, Kingsway Camp, Delhi-110009; Phone: 27233967 Focus Area: Multiple disability.

170. Udaan For The Dis-abled
A-59, Kailash Colony, New Delhi-110048, Phone: 41631140; HQ Phone: 26446978 Focus Area: Children with Cerebral Palsy, Autism, Mentally Challenged or Multiple Handicap

UDAAN—INDIRA AUTISM & CP RESEARCH PROJECT D-93 Amar Colony, Lajpatnagar-4, New Delhi 110024, Phone: 41621137 Focus Area: Medical Intervention in Autism & Cerebral Palsy; one-to-one OT / PT / Speech / Special education / Sensory Integration therapy, Psychological diagnosis and counseling, mHBAT (1.3 ATA Air), rHBOT (1.5 ATA 100 per cent Oxygen), DAN Protocol, MB12, Heavy metal detoxification Contact person: Dr. Arun Mukherjee, Cell 9811157839,
E-mail: arun@udaan.org; Web site: www.udaan.org,

171. Very Special Arts India
C-418 Defence Colony, New Delhi-110024; Phone: 24615243, 26134983 Focus Area: Multiple Disability.
172. Vidya Bharti Foundation
Shankar Vidya Kendra, opp. C-Block Market, Paschim Marg, New Delhi-110057; Phone: 26143128, 25692983 Focus Area: Mentally ill.
173. Vimhans (Vidya Sagar Institute of Mental Health and Neuro Sciences) No 1, Institutio-nal Area, Nehru Nagar, New Delhi-110065; Phone: 26310510, 26310520
e-mail: vimhans@vsnl.com Focus Area: Orthopaedicaly handicapped; Cerebral palsy; Learning disabilities; Neurological.
174. Vocational Rehabilitation Center for Handicapped I.T.I. Campus, Pusa, New Delhi-110012; Phone: 25788780 Focus Area: Multiple disability.
175. Well Being Counseling & Health Center
U-158, Vats Complex (near subway), Main Vikas Marg, Shakarpur, New Delhi-110092; Phone: 22440556 Focus Area: Mentally retarded; Orthopaedically handicapped; Hearing impaired; Slow learner; Autism.
176. Ymca Institute for Special Education YMCA,
Nizamuddin East, New Delhi-110013; Phone: 24699405, 24624061 Fax: 24634209 Focus Area: Mentally retarded.
177. Jingle Bells Academy,
S-438, School Block, Part-II, Shakarpur, Delhi;
Email: anju_70gupta@yahoo.co.in and jinglebells_2002@yahoo.co.in Contact no: 9811819951, 22482348 Focus area: Inclusive education for MR

Annexure II
Softwares that Help Learning Disabled

1. Creature Antics by Laureate Learning Systems Inc.

Designed for those with severe difficulties, this programme has cast of animated characters helping users to begin learning about cause and effect and turn taking. Similar programmes included Creature Capers, Creature Cartoons, Creature Chorus, Creature features, Creature magic.

Availability: Commercial product
Contact: Laureate Learning Systems, Inc.
Phone: +1-802-655-4755
Fax: +1-802-655-4757
E-mail: customer-service@laureatelearning.com

2. Early Learning I, II, III by Marblesoft.

This programme is designed to let the student have fun learning while requite a minimum amount of time from the teacher or parent. Early Learning I includes 4 activities that teach pre-reading skills, Early Learning II includes 4 activities that teach addition and number sequencing. Early Learning III includes 3 activities that teach subtraction and number comparison.

Availability: Commercial product
Contact: Marblesoft USA
E-mail: mail@marblesoft.com

3. Following Directions: Left and Right by Laureate Learning Systems Inc.

Designed to help those with disabilities and impairments, this programme offers 10 activities to help student learn to follow directions and discriminate between left and right, accessible through keyboard, touch screen or single switch.

Availability: Commercial product
Contact: Laureate Learning Systems Inc.
Phone: +1-802-655-4755
Fax: +1-802-655-4757
E-mail: customer—service@laureatelearning.com

4. Micro—LADs: MicroComputers Language Assessment and Development System by Laureate Learning Systems Inc.

Designed to train 46 basic syntactic structures, this is aimed at the special needs of those with disabilities and impairments, accessible with keyboard, touch screen, single switch or mouse.

Availability: Commercial product
Contact: Laureate Learning Systems Inc.
Phone: +1-802-655-4755
Fax: +1-802-655-4757
E-mail: customer—service@laureatelearning.com

5. Monkeys Jumping on the Bed by Soft Touch Software

This programme combines a favorite preschool song with number and colour activities. Students with cognitive delays respond to upbeat music and interesting sounds. Large graphics help learners focus on the action.

Availability: Commercial product.
Contact: Soft Touch Software USA
Phone: +1-877-763-8868
Fax. +1-661-396-8760
E-mail: support@softtouch.com

6. Teach Me to Talk by Soft Touch Software

Many students have difficulties learning to speak. This programme features several strategies where children learn language through rhyme, rhythm, and repetition.

Availability: Commercial product
Contact: Soft Touch Software USA

Phone: +1-877-763-8868
Fax: +1-661-396-8760
E-mail: support@softtouch.com

7. Co: Writer 4000 by Don Johnston Inc.

Co: Writer is a writing assistant with intelligent word prediction, a productivity tool for those who struggle with writing due to injury, physical limitation, language delay or learning disability. Co: Writer is suitable for all vocabulary levels. And the speech output gives auditory feedback to those who need to hear their words. Co: Writer is a whole—language—writing tool for novel communication and for student with language deficiencies or learning disabilities.

Availability: Commercial product
Contact: Don Johnston Inc USA
Phone: +1-847-526-2682
Fax: +1-847-526-4177
E-mail: info@donjohnston.com

8. Write: OutLoud by Don Johnston Inc.

Write: OutLoud is a flexible and user—friendly talking word processor that offers multisensory learning and positive reinforcement for writers of all ages and ability levels. Write: OutLoud uses CD—quality audio to repeat words, letters and sentences as students type. The auditory feedback is great for students with learning disabilities because they can hear if words are omitted or substituted. Write: OutLoud is a suitable creature writing programme for all ages and especially for students with learning disabilities.

Availability: Commercial product
Contact: Don Johnston Inc. USA
Phone: +1-847-526-2682
Fax: +1-847-526-4177
E-mail: info@donjohnston.com

9. Dyna Vox Mac by Dyna Vox Systems Inc.

Dyna Vox Mac software helps students with disabilities break through the barriers to learn and succeed in the classroom. Dyna Vox software can be used to create dynamically linked communication pages for those with special speech, language and learning needs. Dyna Vox Mac acts as a speech/language therapy tool and also helps turn a Macintosh into an augmentative communication device for the speech disabled.

Availability: Commercial product
Contact: Dyna Vox Systems Inc.
Phone: +1-888-697-7332
E-mail: sales@dynavoxsys.com

10. Weirdkids.com

Contains a site on Autism and Autism—related information such as recommended books and medical information.

Email: shannon@weirdkids.com
http://www.weirdkids.com/autism/index.htm

11. Fast Forword

A software for very young children to build the critical early learning skills. It is recommended as an appropriate tool for children with Autism.
Address: Scientific Learning 300 Frank H. Ogawa Plaza Suite 500

Oakland, CA 94612-2040
Phone: 1-888-665-9707
Fax: 510-444-3580
Email: info@scilearn.com
http://www.fastforword.com

12. Access to Math

An on screen talking math worksheet that guides a student to math solutions. Students with learning disabilities can learn math at their own pace with this programme.

Availability: Commercial product
Contact: Don Johnston Inc USA
Phone: +1-847-526-2682
Fax: +1-847-526-4177
E-mail: info@donjohnston.com

Annexure III
Learning Disabilities Checklist

Domains and Behaviours *Shaded area indicates a characterstics is more likely to apply at that stage of life. Check all that apply.*	Preschool Kindergarten	Grades 1-4	Grades 5-8	High School & Adult
Gross and Fine Motor Skills				
Appears awkward and clumsy, dropping, spilling, or knocking things over				
Has limited success with games and activities that demand eye-hand coordination (i.e., piano lessons, basketball, baseball)				
Has trouble with buttons, hooks, snaps, zippers and trouble learning to tie shoes				
Creates art work that is immature for age				
Demonstrates poor ability to colour or write 'within the lines'				
Grapes pencil awkwardly, resulting in poor handwriting				
Experiences difficulty using small objects or items that demand precion (i.e. legos, puzzle pieces, tweezers, scissors)				
Dislikes and avoids writing and drawing tasks				
Language				
Demonstrates early delays in learning to speak				
Has difficulty modulating voice (i.e. too soft, too loud)				
Has trouble naming people or objects				
Has difficulty staying on topic				
Inserts invented words into conversation				
Has difficulty re-telling what has just been said				
Uses vague, imprecise language and has a limited vocabulary				
Demonstrates slow and halting speech, using lots of fillers (i.e. uh, um, and, you know, so)				

(*Contd.*)

Uses poor grammar or misuses words in conversation				
Mispronounces words frequently				
Confuses words with other that sound similar				
Inserts malapropisms (slips of the tongue) into conversation (i.e., a rolling stone gathers no moths; he was a man of great statue)				
Has difficulty rhyming				
Has limited interest in book or stories				
Has difficulty understanding instructions or directions				
Has trouble understanding idioms, proverbs, colloquialisms, humor, and/or puns (note: take into account regional and cultural factors)				
Hss difficulty with pragmatic skills (i.e., understrands the relationship between speaker and listener, makes inferences based on a speaker's verbal and non-verbal cues				
Reading				
Confuses similar-looking letters and numbers				
Has difficulty recognizing and remembering sight words				
Frequently looses place while reading				
Confuses similar-looking words (i.e., beard/bread)				
Reverses letter order in words (i.e. saw/was)				
Demonstrates poor memory for printed words				
Has weak comprehension of ideas and themes				
Has significant trouble learning to read				
Has trouble naming letters				
Has problems associating letter and sounds, understanding the difference between sounds in words or blending sounds into words				
Guesses a unfamiliar words rather than using word analysis skills				
Read slowly				
Substitutes or leaves out words while reading				
Has poor retention of new vocabulary				
Dislikes and avoids reading or reads reluctantly				

(Contd.)

Written Language				
Dislikes and avoids writing and copying				
Demonstrates delays in learning to copy and write				
Writing is messy and incomplete, with many cross outs and erasures				
Has difficulty remembering shapes of letter and numerals				
Frequently reverses letters, numbers and symbols				
Uses uneven spacing between letters and words, and has trouble staying 'on the line'.				
Copies inaccurately (i.e., confuses similar-looking letters and numbers)				
Spells poorly and inconsistently (i.e., the same word appears differently other places in the same document)				
Has difficulty proffreading and self-correcting work				
Has difficulty preparing outlines and organizing written assignments				
Fails to develop ideas in writing so written work is incomplete and too brief				
Expresses written ideas in a disorganized way				
Math				
Has difficulty with simple counting and one-to-one correspondence between number symbols and items/objects				
Difficulty mastering number knowledge (i.e. recognition of quantities without counting)				
Has difficulty with learning and memorizing basic addition and substraction facts				
Has difficulty learning strategic counting principles (i.e. by 2,5,10,100)				
Poorly aligns numbers resulting in computation errors				
Has difficuylty estimating quantity (i.e. quantity, value)				
Has difficulty with comparisons (i.e. less than, greater than)				
Has trouble telling time				

(Contd.)

Has trouble lconceptualizing the passage of time				
Has difficulty counting rapidly or making calculations				
Has trouble learning multiplication tables, formulas and rules				
Has trouble interpreting graphs and charts				
Social/Emotional				
Does not pick up on other people's mood/feelings (i.e., may say the wrong thing at the wrong time)				
May not detect or respond appropriately to teasing				
Has difficulty 'joining in' and maintaining positive social status in a peer group				
Has trouble knowing how to share/express feelings				
Has trouble 'getting to the point' (i.e., gets bogges down in details in conversation				
Has difficulty with self-control when frustrated				
Has difficulty dealing with group pressure, embarrassment and unexpected challenges				
Has trouble setting realistic social goals				
Has trouble evaluating personal social strengths and challenges				
Is doubtful own abilitie and is prone to attribute successes to luck or outside influences rather than hard work				
Attention				
Fails to pay close attention to deails or makes, careless mistakes is schoolwork, work, or other activites				
Has difficulty sustaining attention in work tasks or play activities				
Does not follow through on instructions and fails to finish schoolwork, chores, or duties in the workplace				
Has difficulty organizing tasks and activities				
Avoids, dislikes, or is reluctant to engage in tasks that require sustained mental effort such as homework and organizing work tasks				

(Contd.)

Loses things consistently that are necessary for tasks/activities (i.e., toys, school assignments, pencils, books, or tools)				
Is easily distracted by outside influences				
Is forgetful in daily/routine activities				
Other				
Confuses left and right				
Has a poor sense of direction; slow to learn the way around a new place; easily lost or confused in unfamiliar surroundings				
Finds it hard to judge speed and distance (i.e., hard to pay certain games, drive a car)				
Trouble reading charts and maps				
Is disorganized and poor at planning				
Often loses things				
Is slow to learn new games and master puzzles				
Has difficulty lestening and taking notes at the same time				
Performs inconsistently ontasks fromone day to the next				
Has difficulty generalizing (applying) skills from one situation to another				

Source: National Center for Learning, USA.